# THE AUSTRALIAN GUIDE TO BUYING YOUR FIRST HOME

# THE AUSTRALIAN GUIDE TO BUYING YOUR FIRST HOME

HOW TO **INCREASE** YOUR **INCOME**, **MANAGE** YOUR **MORTGAGE** AND GET DEBT-FREE

**ROBBO ROPER**

WILEY

First published 2025 by John Wiley & Sons Australia, Ltd

© Trusted Finance Pty Ltd 2025

All rights reserved, including rights for text and data mining and training of artificial intelligence technologies or similar technologies. Except as permitted under *the Australian Copyright Act 1968* (for example, a fair dealing for the purposes of study, research, criticism or review) no part of this publication may be reproduced, stored in a retrieval system, or transmitted, in any form or by any means, electronic, mechanical, photocopying, recording or otherwise. Advice on how to obtain permission to reuse material from this title is available at http://www.wiley.com/go/permissions.

The right of Rob Roper to be identified as the author of *The Australian Guide to Buying Your First Home* has been asserted in accordance with law.

ISBN: 978-1-394-26834-4

A catalogue record for this book is available from the National Library of Australia

*Registered Office*
John Wiley & Sons Australia, Ltd. Level 4, 600 Bourke Street, Melbourne, VIC 3000, Australia

For details of our global editorial offices, customer services, and more information about Wiley products visit us at www.wiley.com.

Wiley also publishes its books in a variety of electronic formats and by print-on-demand. Some content that appears in standard print versions of this book may not be available in other formats.

Trademarks: Wiley and the Wiley logo are trademarks or registered trademarks of John Wiley & Sons, Inc. and/or its affiliates in the United States and other countries and may not be used without written permission. All other trademarks are the property of their respective owners. John Wiley & Sons, Inc. is not associated with any product or vendor mentioned in this book.

*Limit of Liability/Disclaimer of Warranty*
While the publisher and author have used their best efforts in preparing this work, they make no representations or warranties with respect to the accuracy or completeness of the contents of this work and specifically disclaim all warranties, including without limitation any implied warranties of merchantability or fitness for a particular purpose. No warranty may be created or extended by sales representatives, written sales materials or promotional statements for this work. This work is sold with the understanding that the publisher is not engaged in rendering professional services. The advice and strategies contained herein may not be suitable for your situation. You should consult with a specialist where appropriate. The fact that an organisation, website, or product is referred to in this work as a citation and/or potential source of further information does not mean that the publisher and author endorse the information or services the organisation, website, or product may provide or recommendations it may make. Further, readers should be aware that websites listed in this work may have changed or disappeared between when this work was written and when it is read. Neither the publisher nor author shall be liable for any loss of profit or any other commercial damages, including but not limited to special, incidental, consequential, or other damages.

Information and data sourced from government websites were current at the time of the writing of this Work. Please be mindful that this data may be subject to change. This book outlines general advice only. It should not replace individual, independent, personal financial advice.

Cover design by Alex Ross Creative
Cover photo: Grace Vivien Photography

Set in Bembo Std 12.5/16.5pt, Straive, Chennai, India.

*For my wife Grace. Thank you for your endless support.
The best thing about this life is building it with you.*

# CONTENTS

Introduction ... ix

## Part I | Take control of your income ... 1

1 | Aim for above average ... 3
2 | How expensive is your life? ... 19
3 | Increase your income ... 37
4 | What are you worth? ... 53

## Part II | Buy your first home ... 73

5 | How much can you borrow? ... 75
6 | How much do you need in savings? ... 93
7 | What should you look for in a home loan? ... 147
8 | What type of home should you buy? ... 169

## Part III | Get debt-free ... 191

9 | Manage your mortgage ... 193
10 | Achieve financial flexibility ... 211

Conclusion: The secret to sustaining a financially flexible life ... 235

Index ... 241

# INTRODUCTION

In my 20s I put myself in a shitload of debt. It led to the biggest breakdown of my life.

Here's what happened.

In 2014, my wife and I bought a home that pushed us to the limit of what we could afford. We had the dream of renovating a run-down, 1960s home into our very own version of a *'Block-worthy'* dream house. If you're an avid *The Block* viewer like we are, you'll understand where we were coming from.

Our strategy was simple. As we continued to climb the corporate ladder in our respective careers, our incomes were expected to increase. Then, once our home went up in value, we would increase our mortgage to release the funds required to complete the renovation. Plan sorted!

However, after a year of living in the house we had a grim moment of realisation. House prices across Perth, Western Australia, had declined. In our suburb, in particular, house prices were down over 5 per cent. Since we bought the house with only a 5 per cent deposit, we now owned a home valued the same as our outstanding mortgage. In the eyes of the bank, our loan-to-value ratio (LVR) was above their 'maximum lending guidelines'. Our refinance plans were no longer viable.

# Learning from my mistakes

I became obsessed with television shows like *Grand Designs*, *Fixer Upper* and *House Hunters*. These shows fuelled my desire to renovate. A daily reminder to keep up with the Joneses.

We must have been talking about it nonstop because one day my wife's parents made us an offer we couldn't refuse. They were willing to increase the mortgage on their own home to fund our renovation as long as we could afford the increase in repayments on their home loan. (I know what you're thinking, and yes, I felt very fortunate to have such generous in-laws.)

We accepted their offer, but with variable home loan interest rates sitting at around 5.5 per cent per annum, and the fact we now had two mortgages on the one property, we elected for the 'renovation mortgage' to be interest only (IO). This strategy reduced our monthly repayments, maximising our cash flow, but it meant the mortgage balance would not decrease over time. We were clinging onto the hope that we could refinance our own mortgage based on the increased value of our renovated home and pay my in-laws back the renovation mortgage in full.

We pushed ourselves to the brink of what we could afford. Every single cent mattered. Then, just like in any home building show you've ever seen, the renovation went over budget. The only way to continue the renovation was to borrow more money from my in-laws. This pushed us beyond what we could afford and, to rub salt into the wound, house prices in Perth continued to plummet. The debt was suffocating. Questions kept circling around in my head:

- What if we can't finish the renovation?
- What if it's worth even less than when we started?
- What if the bank won't let us refinance?
- What if property values keep going down?
- How am I going to pay back my in-laws?
- What will they think of me?
- Do we cut our losses, scrap the rest of the renovation and try to sell what we have—walking away with a debt while being forced back into the rental market—or do we brainstorm a way to create additional income?

You get the gist. It was make or break.

## My turning point

The thought of losing our home was debilitating. As this feeling grew, it became harder for us to come up with a way to generate any additional income. We felt trapped.

I was working fulltime as a high-school teacher and one afternoon, after all the students left, I sat in my classroom and sobbed. I had just calculated that we would be left with a debt of over $200 000 if we tried to sell our home. At that exact moment I received an email from a parent of one of my students wondering if I could tutor their older sibling.

Out of the blue, a viable side hustle had crystalised. It meant working after hours, but in addition to our full-time jobs, it might just be enough to get us over the line. I started marketing my services in local community groups on Facebook. One student turned into two, then three, then suddenly I was tutoring 10 students per week.

I was now working more than 50 hours a week, but that debilitating feeling had dissipated. I could see the light at the end of the tunnel. We were able to finish the renovations and achieved a bank valuation of our property above what we expected. This meant we were able to refinance our mortgage and pay back my in-laws in full.

But I hadn't anticipated the dramatic increase in repayments now that we were forced to pay principal and interest (P&I) on our home loan.

That feeling of suffocation was rearing its ugly head again. But this time it wasn't debilitating. I had already proven to myself I knew how to take control of my income. This made me rethink my tutoring side hustle:

How could I generate even more income?

By restructuring how I delivered the tuition, my business quadrupled in size, growing to over 40 students. Life was good.

For the first time in years, our income was paying our expenses and leaving us with some savings.

To add to our happiness, one day after work, my wife announced she was pregnant.

After feeling pure joy for a few days, that familiar feeling returned. I felt choked by the thought that our income was going to be almost halved once my wife's paid maternity period finished. We were finally comfortable and now this beautiful, but also completely unknown, variable was turning our financial stability upside down.

If you're about to start a family, these are the questions you need to be asking yourself before you make any massive financial decisions:

- How will you continue to afford this life if you have kids?

- What will your life look like? How long will you be living on one salary? How expensive is day care?

- What will this mean in terms of your happiness?

During our renovation, it was questions like these that collided to create a tornado of self-doubt, anxiety and depression. But that financial pressure cooker of a situation forced me to adopt a different mindset. In *Rich Dad Poor Dad,* Robert Kiyosaki explains that he forbids himself from saying, 'I can't afford this'.

He replaces this statement with, 'How can I afford this?'

I know it sounds simple. I remember standing in Big W reading the first few pages of Kiyosaki's book, thinking there's no way something so simple could have an impact. But this strategy completely reshaped my mindset. When I ask myself this question, rather than make a statement, it opens and challenges my mind. Like a seedling growing every day, looking for the light, I'm constantly trying to find a viable solution to my problems. (Try it for yourself—it's powerful.)

I had 9 months to figure things out. So, while I was still working fulltime as a teacher, I took our tutoring business to the next level. I leased an office space and employed my first staff member. Over the next year our team grew to six teachers tutoring over 90 students a week. Between the business and my full-time job, we were doing so well that my wife didn't need to return to work after her maternity leave.

But there was a hard pill to swallow: I was working over 65 hours a week. I was tired. The only thing keeping me going was knowing that our son had his mum by his side 100 per cent of the time—which, in my opinion, was worth every working second.

As the business grew to 15 teachers and over 180 students, it was finally time to reduce my workload. At the start of 2020, I scaled down to around 30 hours a week, and only teaching one day a week. Then, 3 weeks later, we found out baby number two was on the way. But this time I felt prepared. Everything was already in place to handle another little rugrat.

Then COVID happened.

## My breakdown

The impact that COVID had on our tutoring business was devastating. Our income was reduced by 90 per cent due to the lockdown procedures forcing us to shut our doors. It all happened so fast. One week I was able to fully support my family, the next I couldn't even make the mortgage repayment. This prompted my first ever breakdown.

I felt hollow.

The weight of all those years spent working over 60 hours a week to pay for the financial decisions we made in our 20s came crashing down on me all at once.

How long is life going to be like this?

How long can we survive?

I can't afford this!

I was stuck, deep down in that dark hole again. Struggling to see a way out. Weeks went by and the feeling of desperation only grew. But this time my wife was the one holding the torch.

'You've done this before, and you can do it again,' she said.

'How *can* we afford this?' I asked myself.

Trusting that she believed in my ability to provide for our family, regardless of what was going on in the world, was empowering.

Her confidence gave me the resilience I needed to push through and find a solution.

COVID completely rewired me. I was now focused on wrapping my family's lifestyle in a suit of armour. Luckily, due to Western Australia's prompt border closure (which reduced the initial outbreak of COVID in 2020, allowing businesses to reopen after approximately 8 weeks—much sooner than other states), our tutoring business survived. But I was fixated on generating alternative income streams.

I'm sure someone in your life has told you to 'find a job you're passionate about'. But what they don't tell you is that passion isn't a starting point. It's a result. Entrepreneur and leadership expert Simon Sinek said, 'When we work hard at something we don't believe in, we become stressed. When we work hard at something we do believe in, we become passionate'. I already knew that I was passionate about education. After spending 10 years teaching and 3 years building my tutoring business, I knew that whatever I did next needed to revolve around education.

The trials and tribulations of our renovation journey fuelled my desire to complete a mortgage-broking qualification, and just after the birth of our second son, Trusted Finance was born. But as our family grew, so did the number of hours I spent working. I was now split between teaching, the tutoring business and Trusted Finance. While working over 75 hours per week, I took solace in the fact that I genuinely loved what I was doing. That schedule left me with 44 free 'awake' hours per week. With most of those hours spent playing dad, much fewer spent playing husband and even fewer left for myself, I wished that someone had taught me how to take control of my income, set sustainable budgets and forecast the impact of having kids before we bought our first home.

After I started Trusted Finance, I realised something: there are thousands of people out there who could learn from my mistakes. So, I started making content on social media, sharing my journey and educating Australians about the home-buying journey. After a year I had gained over 200 000 followers on TikTok, making me the most followed financial educator in Australia. In a relatively short period of time, I became classified as an expert on first-home buying. Despite the fact I was helping thousands of people buy their first home, I couldn't help but feel like an imposter. In these moments I would go back to 2014, when I was making financial decision after financial decision without anyone warning me of the potential consequences. In those moments of self-doubt, I would repeat this mantra:

*My journey is worth sharing.*

*I have been in your shoes.*

*I can help you buy your first home.*

*I can help you avoid financial stress.*

Through helping as many of my followers as possible, my business evolved. I now connect home buyers with the best mortgage brokers, investment brokers and building brokers all over Australia. At the time of writing, in July of 2024, more than

40 000 home buyers have been connected to brokers via my website www.trustedfinance.loans. I have been, and continue to be, blown away by the support of my 1.3 million followers on social media and hope they know that this book is inspired by their desire to provide for their families.

## How this book will benefit you

As you've just observed, I made countless mistakes when buying my first home. Mistakes that severely affected my mental health. I've learned from these, used strategies to create sustainable budgets, climbed the corporate ladder and built successful businesses to take control of my income. And I balance all of this with being a husband and father. This journey has made me passionate about helping people buy their first home, avoid financial stress and provide for their families. Since you picked up this book, I'm guessing you want to be supported too.

In the pages that follow I will provide a step-by-step plan for buying your first home. As you might have already figured out, I did things in the wrong order. First, I bought a home; then, I tried to budget. When that didn't work out, I desperately tried to increase my income. This is what caused my financial stress.

But this book isn't just the ultimate guide to buying your first home in Australia. It's a roadmap to gaining financial flexibility for you and your family. Each new phase of life poses different challenges. Financial flexibility is about balancing your spending today with your investments into your future. It means that you're investing enough of your income into owning a home, mortgage free, and producing future passive income streams that will enable you to retire years before you gain access to your superannuation. Achieving financial flexibility will release you from the burden of traditional employment while you're still young enough to enjoy the fruits of your labour.

In part I, I'm going to teach you what I wish someone had taught me when I started my home-buying journey: how to take control of your income. By learning how to create a sustainable budget, in line with increasing your hourly rate, you'll be able to save a house deposit while the dream of owning a home is still alive.

The information in part II will save you tens of thousands of dollars in upfront costs and fees. There's an art to buying a home in Australia. Taking advantage of first home buyer incentives, utilising stamp duty exemptions and considering guarantor home loans could result in you buying your first home years earlier than you ever anticipated.

Part III of this book is arguably the most important: how to get debt free as soon as possible. At the age of 36, I made the final repayment on my mortgage. That home loan—the one that caused all that stress in my 20s—is finally paid off. I'm going to teach you how to implement simple strategies that will shave years off the life of your mortgage and save you hundreds of thousands of dollars in interest.

Buying a home and becoming debt free is the key to surviving your retirement. But gaining financial flexibility is the key to enjoying it. In the final chapter of this book, you will create your very own financial flexibility roadmap. I'll share with you how I plan to retire before the age of 50 and live off my passive income, how I plan to maximise my super fund in the lead-up to retirement and the steps I've put in place to help my children buy their first home 20 years from now.

To get the most out of this book you need to reflect on each phase of the journey and explore all your options. I have included a reflection task and an 'Explore your options' activity in each chapter to help you understand your financial position, improve your mindset around your finances and open your eyes to the possibilities available to you.

In each reflection task, you will be guided through a self-analysis designed to highlight your specific areas for growth. The 'Explore your options' activity will show you how to achieve this growth by following a number of possible pathways.

This book is designed to be highlighted, dog-eared, written in and doodled on. By the time you're finished, it will become a first home buying guide and roadmap to financial flexibility that's specific to you.

To show you that you're not alone, I've collated 10 home-buyer journeys in the form of case studies—one at the end of each chapter. They are based on the contexts, incomes, liabilities and goals of the home buyers that my mortgage broker referral partners have supported to achieve property ownership.

To help you get your head around some of the terms and their acronyms related to buying your first home, here's a list of the ones I'll be referring to in this book. You can flick back to this page any time and remind yourself of what each acronym refers to at a glance:

- Australian Bureau of Statistics (ABS)
- Family Home Guarantee (FHG)
- First Home Buyer Guarantee (FHBG)
- First Home Owner Grant (FHOG)
- Higher Education Contribution Scheme (HECS)
- Higher Education Loan Program (HELP)
- Household Expenditure Measure (HEM)
- interest only (IO)
- key performance indicators (KPIs)
- lenders mortgage insurance (LMI)
- loan-to-value ratio (LVR)
- principal and interest (P&I)
- principal place of residence (PPR)

- Regional First Home Buyer Guarantee (RFHBG)

- Situation, Action, Outcome (SAO)

Okay, let's get into it. The earlier you buy your first home, the younger you'll be when it's completed paid off.

# PART I

# Take CONTROL of YOUR INCOME

# 1 | Aim for ABOVE AVERAGE

Let's begin with some stats.

In 2024, the average age of a first home buyer in Australia was 36. In 1984 the average age was 24. An average house today is worth eight times the average income. Back then, it was only four times.

Over the past 40 years the property market has outpaced annual income at such a rate that it has changed the family dynamic for most Australians. Long gone are the days where a family could thrive on an average single income. Instead, most families are making the tough decision to put their children in day care so that both parents can work to cover housing and living expenses.

ABS statistics show that, across Australia, in 2024 the median income was $68 000 per year before tax. This figure includes all work types: fulltime, part time and casual. The median full-time income was $83 000 per year before tax. Where you sit on the income spectrum will determine whether you can buy a house, townhouse, unit or apartment for your first home. In fact, it will determine whether you can buy a property at all.

Most first home buyers today are limited by how much the bank will let them borrow for a home loan. This is called your 'home loan borrowing power' (also known as your 'home loan serviceability'). A bank will calculate your serviceability by comparing your income to your living expenses as well as liabilities such as personal loans, student loans and credit cards.

By the time you've finished reading this book, you'll have created your home buying plan using a strategy specific to you, designed to help you take control of your income, buy your first home and manage your mortgage to create financial flexibility. But before I guide you on this journey, it's important that you understand what type of income you need to earn to buy a home in your city. You need to set realistic expectations so that your goal of home ownership is achievable.

Approach this chapter with an open mind. It's all about options. Every statistic you learn in this chapter should be the fuel that inspires you to keep learning. To keep researching. To act and to change your circumstances.

To create financial flexibility, you need to consider properties in all states in Australia and be open to building a career across a range of industries.

## The average income vs the average house

Before we investigate the type of home you could buy, we first need to unpack your potential borrowing power. How does your income affect the amount a bank will let you borrow for a home loan?

Table 1.1 outlines your borrowing power based on a variable home loan interest rate of 6.5 per cent per year. Banks are constantly adjusting their home loan variable interest rates. As of April 2024, most banks are offering a variable rate of around 6.5 per cent. The higher the interest rate, the less a bank will let you borrow for a home.

It's important that you research current interest rates as you consider the income vs borrowing power figures in table 1.1. For our purposes here, we will assume you don't have any personal loans, student loans or credit cards. The banks refer to these as 'liabilities' and having any or all of them will decrease your maximum home loan borrowing power. (I will discuss how to reduce the impact of these liabilities in chapter 5. For now, let's focus on your income.)

**Table 1.1: your borrowing power on a variable home loan interest rate of 6.5 per cent p.a.**

| Annual income (before tax) | Monthly living expenses (excluding rent) | Maximum borrowing power (at 6.5% p.a. interest rate) |
|---|---|---|
| $50 000 | $1700 | $212 000 |
| $60 000 | $1700 | $275 000 |
| $68 000 (Australian median income — all work types) | $1700 | $314 000 |
| $70 000 | $1800 | $327 000 |
| $80 000 | $1800 | $382 000 |
| $83 000 (Australian full-time median income) | $1800 | $401 000 |

*(continued)*

**Table 1.1: your borrowing power on a variable home loan interest rate of 6.5 per cent p.a. (*cont'd*)**

| Annual income (before tax) | Monthly living expenses (excluding rent) | Maximum borrowing power (at 6.5% p.a. interest rate) |
|---|---|---|
| $90 000 | $2000 | $434 000 |
| $100 000 | $2100 | $487 000 |
| $110 000 | $2200 | $535 000 |
| $120 000 | $2300 | $593 000 |
| $130 000 | $2400 | $625 000 |
| $140 000 | $2600 | $679 000 |
| $150 000 | $2700 | $727 000 |
| $160 000 | $2800 | $760 000 (median dwelling value across Australia in 2024) |
| $170 000 | $2900 | $821 000 |
| $180 000 | $3000 | $859 000 |
| $190 000 | $3200 | $901 000 |
| $200 000 | $3400 | $930 000 |

Moderate living expenses were used here based on the HEM guidelines used by many lenders.
*Source*: Australian Bureau of Statistics. (2015–16). Household Expenditure Survey, Australia: Summary of Results. ABS; Finder. 'HEM Living Expenses: How are they calculated by lenders?' 23 August 2024.

Across Australia the median dwelling value is $760 000. To be approved for a $760 000 home loan (borrowing at 95 per cent of a home costing $800 000), as a single applicant—with no dependants, no personal loans, credit cards or liabilities—you would need an income of $160 000. This is just under double the full-time median income in Australia and almost two-and-a-half times the median income across all job types. This is a harsh reality check. If you're earning an average Australian income, you will not be able to buy an average Australian house.

Outside of winning the lotto, this leaves you with three options:

1. Find a partner and buy a home using your joint income.

2. Buy a cheaper home.

3. Increase your income.

For most people, the path of least resistance is to buy a home once there are two incomes so that they have enough borrowing power. Most people choose this path because it results in purchasing a home that's either larger in size, features a more desirable layout, is in a better location or is on a bigger block. While this option provides the best short-term solution, it can become problematic if you decide to have children and lose some or all of the primary caregiver's income.

If you're expecting a future drop in income, you may choose to buy a cheaper home instead. For decades, this was possible. However, in some cities around Australia—like Sydney, for example—you'd be lucky to find a studio apartment selling for less than $325 000. Since the maximum borrowing power of a median income earner of $68 000 is only $314 000 (bearing in mind that this doesn't take into consideration liabilities such as personal loans, student loans and credit cards), this means at least 50 per cent of Australians are unable to buy a house in Sydney. And with a handful of apartments available at this price point it's safe to say that buying a home in Sydney of any type is unaffordable for the average Australian.

However, Sydney doesn't represent all of Australia. There are more affordable locations in rural New South Wales and other major cities. Table 1.2 gives you a summary of the median dwelling value across all capital cities as of 1 February 2024. Dwellings include houses, townhouses, units and apartments.

Table 1.2: the median dwelling value across all capital cities as at 1 February 2024

| City | Median dwelling value | Income required for this borrowing power at 6.5% p.a. variable with no liabilities |
|---|---|---|
| Sydney | $1 122 439 | $240 000 |
| Melbourne | $777 250 | $163 000 |
| Brisbane | $796 818 | $165 000 |
| Adelaide | $721 376 | $149 000 |
| Perth | $676 823 | $140 000 |
| Hobart | $651 807 | $135 000 |
| Darwin | $501 520 | $105 000 |
| Canberra | $842 971 | $175 000 |
| Combined capitals | $836 013 | $174 000 |
| Combined regionals | $605 085 | $122 000 |
| National | $759 437 | $160 000 |

Source: CoreLogic.

As you can see, Sydney is an outlier. However, the other capital cities are catching up. As at 1 February 2024, Perth and Brisbane have experienced more than 14 per cent annual growth in dwelling prices. My fear is that over a long enough time horizon, all cities will become unaffordable for the average Australian.

This is why you need to put a plan in place to become above average now, while there are still affordable options available.

I'm regularly asked the question, 'When is the best time to buy?'

My answer is always the same: 'It's not about timing the market. It's about time in the market'.

Let's explore some options.

 **EXPLORE YOUR OPTIONS**

## What kind of home can you afford?

Answer the questions below about your own financial circumstances.

- What is your annual income before tax?
- If you intend to buy a home with your partner, what is your combined annual income before tax?
- Using the figures in table 1.1 (see page 5), what is your maximum home loan borrowing power? If your borrowing power is based on your and your partner's income, use your combined annual income before tax.

In later chapters we will analyse your financial situation in more detail. For now, let's research the type of home you could buy based on your maximum home loan borrowing power. When researching properties, I like to use *www.realestate.com.au*. You can download the app on your phone and easily search for properties in different states using a range of filters.

*(continued)*

1. For this task, we're going to filter based on location and maximum home value. Research the information below three times to compare the types of homes you could afford to buy across three capital cities in Australia based on your current income.

    - City
    - Type of home (house, townhouse, unit or apartment)
    - Name of suburb
    - Number of bedrooms
    - Number of bathrooms
    - Size of block (square metres)
    - Distance to CBD
    - Sale price
    - Would you be happy to live in a property like this? Why / Why not?

2. Now I want you to research the same three cities, this time looking for a more desirable, more expensive home. This is a home you wouldn't be able to afford without increasing your income. However, it may be in a better location, closer to your friends, family and work, larger in size or on a bigger block of land than the home you researched above.

    - City
    - Type of home (house, townhouse, unit or apartment)
    - Name of suburb
    - Number of bedrooms
    - Number of bathrooms

- Size of block (square metres)
- Distance to CBD
- Sale price
- What are the top three features of this home?

After researching properties for sale across a range of capital cities in Australia I'm sure you've come to realise there are still some affordable pockets left. However, I appreciate your desire to live in a particular city. This decision might be based on the city itself, family and friends who live in that city or the opportunities for career progression. In this case, it probably means you need to increase your income to buy the ideal property in your desired location.

There are more opportunities today than ever before to increase your income. You could climb the corporate ladder, start your own side hustle or completely change industries. I want these statistics to inspire you to act now. To make you realise that taking control of your income now will enable you to buy your first home while it's still viable. It will enable you and your family to lead the lifestyle you deserve, before that lifestyle becomes completely out of reach.

## Finding an industry that suits your income goals

If you're earning an average income, you're underpaid. Don't get me wrong: you might be adequately paid based on your responsibilities and skill level compared to others in a similar role, but half of all working adults in Australia earn more than you. This statistic should motivate you. Think about how many jobs there are that pay more than what you're currently earning. The thought is overwhelming. There are so many industries, so many occupations, so many possible career pathways.

To create an action plan, we need to do some research. Table 1.3 compares the highest paid jobs that either require a degree or don't require a degree.

**Table 1.3: the highest paid jobs requiring and not requiring a degree**

| Degree required | | No degree required | |
|---|---|---|---|
| Occupation | Average income p.a. | Occupation | Average income p.a. |
| Surgeon, anaesthetist, internal medicine specialist | $304 000–$394 000 | Construction manager | $154 000 |
| Financial dealer | $275 000 | ICT manager | $123 000 |
| Psychiatrist | $235 000 | Project manager | $122 000 |
| Legal professional | $188 000 | HR manager | $115 000 |
| Mining engineer | $184 000 | FIFO (fly-in, fly-out) truck driver | $115 000 |

Source: *Upskilled*. 'Australia's top 10 highest paying jobs you don't need a degree for'; Monarch Institute. 'The top 15 highest paying careers in Australia'. 25 April 2024.

If you read through table 1.3 and thought, 'Robbo, there's no way I'm becoming a doctor — what a waste of time!', I want you to realise that this table represents a snapshot of the top average incomes by occupation. For half of these jobs, you need a university degree and further training while on the job. For the other half, no degree is required, but you would still need a certain level of qualification. For most FIFO truck driver positions, you need to hold a heavy rigid (HR) drivers licence. All the other occupations in the 'no degree required' list are at managerial level. This means, in addition to initial qualifications, most employees in these roles have worked their way up the corporate ladder in similar industries.

Your goal in your 20s and 30s should be to experiment with as many different industries as possible. Think of your employability as a bouquet of flowers. Each flower represents a skill that you bring to your employer. Some jobs, particularly at entry level, only give you the opportunity to learn and refine a few skills. A bouquet containing only one flower isn't very valuable. A bouquet containing a few of the same flowers isn't much better. Your goal is to fill that bouquet with as many different flowers as possible. You want it to be jam-packed with so many valuable skills that any employer would jump at the chance to buy it. Let's figure out what types of flowers you should collect for your bouquet.

 **REFLECT**

## Situation, Action, Outcome (SAO)

According to *Indeed*—one of the largest job-listing websites in the world—employers share a preference for eight skills, regardless of industry. These eight skills are:

1. Decision making
2. Multitasking
3. Problem-solving

*(continued)*

4. Collaboration
5. Communication
6. Self-motivation
7. Empathy
8. Leadership.

To maximise your chances of gaining a promotion, it's important for you to reflect on all eight skills. How have you developed these skills in your working life so far?

For each skill, describe a situation (S) you've faced, either as an individual or as part of a team. Then recount the actions (A) you took to solve this problem. Finally, describe how your actions positively impacted your workplace — in other words, what was the outcome (O)? The more specific you can be, the better. These situations can come from any job you've had in the past. However, recent examples will have more weight in the eyes of a future employer.

The Situation, Action, Outcome (SAO) method of writing a resume is an effective way of showcasing your skills to a potential employer. Your goals of home ownership and becoming financially flexible are solely reliant on your ability to generate a certain income. In the chapters that follow we're going to use your SAO examples to increase the likelihood that you can obtain a higher paying job. With the cost of dwellings continuing to climb, I hope you now understand the importance of generating an above-average income just so you can buy an average home. In fact, in some cities an above-average income may be required to buy even the cheapest home.

# CASE STUDY

## Chloe's home-buying journey

In August 2022, at the age of 28, Chloe was ready to buy her first home. She had her eye on a four-bedroom, two-bathroom home built in 1984 roughly 25 minutes from the Perth CBD. The asking price for the house was $580 000. Despite having enough saved to purchase the home, Chloe hesitated. Back in 2022, she had predicted that interest rates would rise, causing house prices to fall over the next few years. Chloe decided to spend a portion of her deposit on travel, exploring Europe in 2022 and the United States in 2023, leaving her with a smaller house deposit.

Unfortunately for Chloe, her prediction was half right. Interest rates did increase, with standard variable home loan interest rates climbing from 2.7 per cent to 6.5 per cent, but house prices in Perth also skyrocketed. The 2024 housing market was vastly different from 2022 and increased interest rates had a massive impact on her borrowing power.

### Chloe's financial snapshot

| | | | |
|---|---|---|---|
| Annual before-tax income | $92 000 | Monthly living expenses | $2000 |
| Job title | Planning officer | Total credit card limits | $1000 |
| Total savings | $25 000 | Monthly personal loan repayments | $0 |
| Eligible for government support | Yes: FHBG | Monthly student debt repayments | $384 |
| Parent guarantor | No | Residency status | Australian citizen |

(*continued*)

## Chloe's outcome

Chloe's maximum borrowing power of $419 000 didn't leave her with the option of buying a house in a similar location to where she was looking in 2022. Her reduced savings of $25 000 also meant she needed to secure a full stamp duty exemption (I'll explain this in chapter 6) to enter the housing market.

Chloe decided to buy a townhouse instead after finding a two-bedroom, one-bathroom dwelling 25 minutes from the Perth CBD for $425 000. She utilised the First Home Guarantee (FHBG) to avoid paying lenders mortgage insurance (LMI) and claimed a full stamp duty exemption. (I'll also explain how this grant and LMI work in chapter 6.) Chloe secured a home loan at 95 per cent of the property's value after contributing $24 000 of her savings towards her deposit and the upfront costs. Repayments on the $403 000 mortgage are $576 per week.

# Key takeaways for your home-buying journey

- The 2024 median income in Australia across all income types is $68 000. For a full-time worker, it's $83 000.

- An average house today is worth eight times the average income. Back in 1984, it was only four times the average income.

- To create financial flexibility, you need to consider properties in all states and be open to building a career across a range of industries.

- To buy an average home on an average income, you will most likely have to purchase your home with a partner, purchase a cheaper home or increase your income.

- Purchasing a home is not about timing the market. It's about time in the market.

- Regardless of industry, there are common skills that employers prefer. Refining these skills in your current workplace and learning to communicate how you utilise them will increase the likelihood you achieve the above average income you will need to buy your first home and give your family the lifestyle they deserve.

# 2 | How EXPENSIVE is your LIFE?

Just recently, I heard a wealthy property investor say that the reason young people are struggling to save for a house deposit is because they have 'champagne taste on a beer budget'. He couldn't be more out of touch.

Throughout the 2021–2022 financial year, Australia experienced 6.59 per cent inflation against wage growth of only 2.6 per cent. This basically means everything became much more expensive compared to our incomes and, as consumers, we've been chasing our tails ever since

'Cost of living' is how much it costs to afford the necessities in life—'necessities' being the key word here. What that boomer property investor didn't take into consideration is that simply existing has become more expensive.

The cost of living can be broken down into the following categories:

- Housing
- Food

- Transportation
- Healthcare
- Utilities.

These categories are classified as 'essential'. There are many factors that influence how much you spend in each of these categories. For example, the average person living in Sydney spends 36 per cent more on housing than someone living in Melbourne. Research conducted by financial comparison site *finder.com.au* identified that an 85-square-metre, fully furnished apartment costs $2508 per month to rent in Sydney, whereas the same-size apartment in a comparable location in Melbourne only costs $1857.

In part II of this book, I'm going to teach you how to calculate your maximum borrowing power and create your home-buying savings target. To maximise the likelihood of achieving this target, we must first investigate ways to minimise your everyday expenses. According to *finder.com.au* the average Australian is spending the largest portion of their income on housing and food. Since these are the big-ticket items when it comes to our expenses, many people make the mistake of focusing solely on how much rent they're paying or on ways to reduce the grocery bill. To create an effective budget, we must first begin by identifying your *non*-essential expenses.

## REFLECT

## Essential vs non-essential

It's time to get out a highlighter, or if you're technologically savvy, you could use the 'mark up' function on your phone. First, you need to log in to your internet banking and download a statement outlining your past 3 months of spending. If you use solely one transaction account, then this one statement should contain all the information you need. If you also use a credit card or several accounts for your everyday expenses, then you'll need to download a 3-month statement for each of these accounts. Your goal here is to categorise your spending habits into 'essential' and 'non-essential'—you can use the following lists as a guide.

Essential expenses include:

- Rent
- Grocery shopping
- Petrol / car maintenance
- Healthcare
- Electricity/water/gas
- Phone/internet

Non-essential expenses include:

- Eating out / having food delivered
- Alcohol
- Smoking-related costs
- Travel
- Streaming services
- Other

*(continued)*

After listing the amount spent for each of your expenses, work out the 3-monthly total for essentials and non-essentials separately and then divide each total by 3 to give you average monthly totals.

Now use the following formula to estimate the percentage of your monthly income that goes towards essential expenses and how much goes towards non-essential expenses:

**Monthly total expenses ÷ monthly after-tax income × 100 = percentage of total income.**

For example, if your monthly total essential expenses add up to $2000 and your monthly after-tax income is $4000, the percentage of your total income spent on essential expenses would be 50%:

**$2000 ÷ $4000 × 100 = 50%**

Once you have determined your current spending habits and contemplated how to reduce each category, you can implement an achievable, sustainable budget. I call this the Basic Budget.

## The Basic Budget

A common budgeting strategy is to separate your spending into three categories: your needs, your wants and your savings. Now that you have identified your essential spending (your needs) and your non-essential spending (your wants), you should be able to easily compare your spending habits against the Basic Budget. To achieve this budget, you should be spending approximately 50 per cent of your income on your needs and 30 per cent on your wants. The remaining 20 per cent should go towards savings, as illustrated in figure 2.1.

*Pie chart showing: Needs 50%, Wants 30%, Savings 20%*

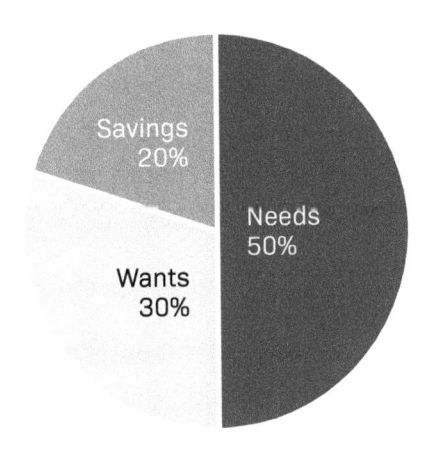

**Figure 2.1: the Basic Budget breakdown**

Find out how far off you are from achieving the Basic Budget breakdown by completing table 2.1. This will reveal your spending habits compared to the Basic Budget.

**Table 2.1: the Basic Budget vs your spending habits**

|  | Basic Budget goal | Your current spending (as a percentage) | How far off are you? (goal minus spending) |
|---|---|---|---|
| **Needs** (essential expenses) | 50% | | |
| **Wants** (non-essential expenses) | 30% | | |
| **Savings** | 20% | | |

If you're not already doing so, is it possible for you to adjust your spending to align with the Basic Budget percentages? Are there any non-essential expenses that could be removed or reduced to achieve a savings target of 20 per cent?

If you've never created a budget in your life, the Basic Budget is a great starting point. Simply being forced to reflect on your spending habits as a percentage of your overall income is a productive way to make informed decisions about your spending. But will this method work for everyone? Unfortunately, no.

Table 2.2 compares a range of incomes to gauge what your needs, wants and spending should be if you want to stick to the Basic Budget.

Table 2.2: how much you should allow for needs, wants and savings on different incomes based on the Basic Budget breakdown

| Yearly income before tax | $70 000 | $100 000 | $130 000 |
|---|---|---|---|
| Monthly income after tax | $4611 | $6249 | $7847 |
| Monthly needs: 50% | $2305.50 | $3124.50 | $3923.50 |
| Monthly wants: 30% | $1383.30 | $1874.70 | $2354.10 |
| Monthly saving: 20% | $922.20 | $1249.80 | $1569.40 |

Due to the cost of living having dramatically increased over the past few years, the minimum amount required to pay for our needs has made it almost impossible for someone earning $70 000 per year to stick to the Basic Budget.

According to the Household Expenditure Measure (HEM) — a tool many banks use to determine someone's average living expenses — a single person living in New South Wales with a 'basic' lifestyle spends $1707 per month on their living expenses plus an additional $2202 per month on rent. This means they are spending $3909 on needs. Based on a monthly after-tax income of $4611, someone earning $70 000 per year would need to set aside 84.78 per cent of their income simply to survive.

If we assume someone earning $100 000 also has a 'basic' lifestyle, then they're spending 62.55 per cent of their income to survive. So how much do you need to earn to adhere to the Basic Budget? Someone earning $130 000 in New South Wales with a 'basic' lifestyle would spend 49.82 per cent of their income on needs based on the HEM.

All of this paints a bleak picture, considering the median full-time annual income across Australia is $84 000.

So how does the average cost of living compare across other states and territories in Australia? Tables 2.3, 2.4 and 2.5 (overleaf) list figures for various lifestyles in all states and territories for a single adult, two adults, and two adults and two children respectively.

**Table 2.3: monthly household expenditure measure for a single adult**

| State | Basic lifestyle expenses + rent | Moderate lifestyle expenses + rent | Lavish lifestyle expenses + rent |
|---|---|---|---|
| NSW | $3909 | $5356 | $7835 |
| ACT | $3676 | $5029 | $7415 |
| NT | $3573 | $4885 | $7229 |
| QLD | $3569 | $4880 | $7223 |
| WA | $3539 | $4838 | $7169 |
| VIC | $3384 | $4621 | $6890 |
| SA | $3369 | $4600 | $6863 |
| TAS | $3312 | $4519 | $6759 |

Table 2.4: monthly household expenditure measure for two adults

| State | Basic lifestyle expenses + rent | Moderate lifestyle expenses + rent | Lavish lifestyle expenses + rent |
|---|---|---|---|
| NSW | $5488 | $7124 | $9793 |
| ACT | $5204 | $6727 | $9283 |
| NT | $5079 | $6551 | $9057 |
| QLD | $5076 | $6546 | $9051 |
| WA | $5039 | $6495 | $8985 |
| VIC | $4851 | $6232 | $8646 |
| SA | $4832 | $6206 | $8613 |
| TAS | $4762 | $6108 | $8487 |

Table 2.5: monthly household expenditure measure for two adults and two children

| State | Basic lifestyle expenses + rent | Moderate lifestyle expenses + rent | Lavish lifestyle expenses + rent |
|---|---|---|---|
| NSW | $6711 | $8560 | $11442 |
| ACT | $6371 | $8084 | $10829 |
| NT | $6220 | $7874 | $10559 |
| QLD | $6216 | $7867 | $10551 |
| WA | $6172 | $7806 | $10471 |
| VIC | $5946 | $7490 | $10066 |
| SA | $5924 | $7459 | $10026 |
| TAS | $5840 | $7341 | $9875 |

# Lifestyle creep

Hopefully you were able to find some areas where you can cut back on spending after working through the previous section.

The other possibility for saving more money, as we saw earlier, is to earn more. You might think that increasing your income will result in more savings, but that's not always the case thanks to a phenomenon called lifestyle creep.

Lifestyle creep is usually described as overspending on non-essential items as your income increases. Many people think lifestyle creep refers to a person treating themselves to a Louis Vuitton handbag or a brand-new Rolex — and they're not wrong. Others choose to treat themselves, their family or friends with lavish gifts by engaging in retail therapy, booking an overseas holiday or subscribing to every streaming service out there. But for most, it's the small 'life upgrades' that add up.

When a family of three becomes a family of four, if their income allows for it, they might justify upgrading the family home and renting a three-bedroom dwelling instead of a two-bedder. And they classify this as essential. But would they have moved if the family's income had stayed the same? Another family might justify moving to a more convenient suburb with a greater range of amenities that's a shorter distance from work. But if they're only moving because a recent pay rise makes them feel they can afford to, isn't this just lifestyle creep?

Let me be clear. I want you to enjoy your life, but my philosophy is that the short-term gain associated with lifestyle creep is not worth the long-term pain of not owning a home. I don't want you to still be renting when you reach the age of retirement. If you don't create financial flexibility during the working phase of life, you risk becoming a burden to your children during your later years. One of the biggest gifts you can give your adult kids, as they enter the phase of starting their own families, is the comfort of knowing you are financially independent.

So, let's dive a bit deeper into the signs of lifestyle creep.

## Six signs of lifestyle creep

Here are six areas to consider keeping tabs on if you want to avoid lifestyle creep.

1. *Social life:* you're going out more often, choosing more expensive locations and approaching these social events without a maximum spending figure in mind.

2. *Shopping habits:* to reduce the percentage of your income you're spending on 'wants', it's important to search for bargains. The moment you start buying items regardless of price—especially if the items are sold at more competitive prices elsewhere—you've adopted a lifestyle creep mindset.

3. *Transport:* this is the most common upgrade when people start earning more money. Public transport usually upgrades to a car and parking fees, and car owners often upgrade their cars with the help of a personal loan.

4. *Holidays:* there is a direct correlation between holiday destination and lifestyle creep. What might have started off as camping twice a year has turned into camping plus an overseas holiday.

5. *Household comforts:* is your house always at the perfect temperature? Was there a time when you wore a jumper inside the house instead of turning on the heater? Are

you opting for Uber Eats more often than cooking up what's left over in the fridge?

6. *Entertainment:* the average number of video-on-demand subscriptions per household in Australia is 3.4. A report by Kantar states that Aussies are more likely to switch between services than to stack subscriptions. How many hours per week are you watching each of your video-on-demand services? Your answer might prompt you to cancel a subscription for a period of time.

# Create your money goal

The percentage targets of the Basic Budget are fixed, regardless of your income. This means that if you're on a lower salary, a higher proportion of your income will need to be spent on needs; on a higher salary, a larger percentage should be allocated to savings. The variable in the equation, outside of your income, is your wants. You need to figure out what proportion of your wants you're willing to sacrifice in order to increase the proportion of your savings.

This is where your money goal comes into play. Since you've purchased a book titled *The Australian Guide to Buying Your First Home*, I'm assuming your house deposit is high up on your money goal list. Later in the book, I'm going to teach you how to calculate exactly how much you need in savings to buy your first home.

To create your budget, we're going to assume a savings target of $30 000 (this is your money goal). The biggest influence on the proportions of your budget is time. How long will it take you to achieve this money goal?

## EXPLORE YOUR OPTIONS

# Calculate your money goal time frame

1. Use the prompts below to calculate how many months it would take you to save $30 000. Base your calculations on your current spending habits, which we worked out earlier in this chapter. Here's an example based on someone earning $85 000 and being able to save 8 per cent of their after-tax income.

    Monthly income after tax: $ _5580_

    Monthly savings: $ _447_

    Monthly savings as a percentage (savings ÷ income × 100): _8_ %

    Months to save $30 000 ($30 000 ÷ monthly savings): _68_ months

2. How could you reduce your wants and increase the percentage of your income that you save? Once you have a new savings target, work out your new savings percentage. The example is based on doubling your savings target.

    New savings percentage: _16_ %

    New monthly savings amount (new monthly savings percentage ÷ 100 × monthly income after tax): _$894_

    Months to save $30 000 ($30 000 ÷ new monthly savings target): _34_ months

    How many months did you save by increasing your savings target? Did it make a noticeable difference? _I saved 34 months or 2 Years and 10 months._

3. Now let's see what would happen if your needs and wants stayed the same, but you increased your income to increase your monthly savings. You can use the website *www.paycalculator.com.au* to calculate your increased monthly after-tax income.

   Use the formula below to work out how many months it would take you to save $30 000, assuming you're earning an extra $10 000 (before tax) per year. For our example, this would make the pre-tax income $95 000.

   New monthly after-tax income (use www.paycalculator.com.au): *$6149*

   Monthly savings (new monthly after-tax income; original needs and wants based on old income): *$1016*

   New monthly savings percentage (new savings ÷ income × 100): *16.5%*

   Months to save $30 000 ($30 000 ÷ new monthly savings): *30* months

   How many months did you save by increasing your annual gross (that is, before-tax) income by $10 000? Did it make a noticeable difference? *I saved 38 months or 3 years and 2 months.*

4. Okay, since we're on a roll, let's now work out how many months it would take to save $30 000 based on earning an extra $20 000 pre-tax per year. For our example, that would be a pre-tax income of $105 000.

   New monthly income after tax (use www.paycalculator.com.au): *$6713*

   Monthly savings (if your needs and wants stayed the same): *$1580*

   *(continued)*

> New monthly savings percentage (new savings ÷ income × 100): _23.5%_
>
> Months to save $30 000 ($30 000 ÷ new monthly savings): _19_ months
>
> How many months did you save by increasing your pre-tax income by $20 000 per year? Did it make a noticeable difference? _I saved 49 months or 4 years and 1 month._
>
> This task is designed to make you consider how restricting your spending compares to increasing your income. It's important to note, however, that the above calculations assume that your lifestyle doesn't become more expensive as you earn a greater income—that is, don't engage in lifestyle creep.

No matter what type of budget you find on the internet, no matter how the proportions of spending vs saving are sliced or what labels they've been assigned, you've probably come to one conclusion: life has become bloody expensive. So expensive, in fact, that it has become almost impossible for someone on an average Australian income to restrict their spending on essential items to around 50 per cent. Most people on this income are lucky if they can restrict their essential spending to 80 per cent. Many have given up on saving, choosing to spend the remaining 20 per cent on making life worth living.

Let's face it: the dream of home ownership is dying. But it's not dead. Not yet. You still have time on your side. You still have an opportunity to increase your income, find a budget that works for you and save a house deposit. If you're overwhelmed by the idea of increasing your income, then you've come to the right place. The next two chapters will give you the skills and, more importantly, inspire you to create a game plan that will increase your income over time. Let's get stuck into it before it's too late.

## CASE STUDY

## Matt and Sahanika's home-buying journey

Matt and Sahanika, aged 32 and 35 respectively, immigrated from the UK to Australia at the start of 2022. Sahanika joined the Victorian police force and Matt gained employment in the hospitality industry. They immediately applied for permanent residency status in the hopes of taking advantage of the first home buyer benefits. After using all of their savings to fund the move to Australia, Matt and Sahanika's number-one priority was to save a house deposit. To minimise their living expenses, they moved into a share house with another couple, effectively splitting the rent between four people. This allowed them to hit their combined weekly savings target of $370. After a solid three years of savings, Matt and Sahanika had $57 000 to show for it. It was time to break free from the rental trap and start house hunting.

### Matt and Sahanika's financial snapshot

| Matt's annual before-tax income | $55 000 | Parent guarantor | No |
|---|---|---|---|
| Sahanika's annual before-tax income | $90 000 | Monthly living expenses | $1800 |
| Total annual before-tax income | $145 000 | Total credit card limits | $0 |

*(continued)*

| Job titles | Matt: Concierge Sahanika: Police officer | Monthly personal loan repayments | $0 |
|---|---|---|---|
| Total savings | $57 000 | Monthly student debt repayments | $0 |
| Eligible for government support | Yes: RFHBG | Residency status | Both permanent residents |

## Matt and Sahanika's outcome

Matt and Sahanika opted to search for properties valued around their maximum borrowing power of $705 000. After researching for a few weeks, they fell in love with a four-bedroom, two-bathroom house located in Geelong and secured the property for $700 000. Since the home is in a regional area, they were able to utilise the Regional First Home Buyer Guarantee (RFHBG) (I'll explain the RFHBG and LMI in chapter 6), buying the property with only a 5-per-cent deposit and no LMI. However, they did have to pay approximately $27 000 in stamp duty and other upfront charges. They now have a home loan of $665 000 at a variable rate of 6.5 per cent per year with repayments of $970 per week.

# Key takeaways
# for your home-buying journey

- The cost of living continues to outpace wage growth, making it harder for the average Australian to survive, let alone hit a savings target.

- Your expenses can be categorised into essential and non-essential spending. Before you attempt a budget, it's important to analyse your current spending to determine how much you spend in each expense category.

- The Basic Budget is to allocate 50 per cent of your income to 'needs' (essential spending), 30 per cent to 'wants' (non-essential spending) and 20 per cent to 'savings'.

- Based on the HEM, the average Australian would need to earn approximately $130 000 per year before tax to allocate only 50 per cent of their monthly after-tax income to essential spending.

- Reducing your non-essential living expenses will result in more savings, but it probably will not be enough to save for a house deposit in your money goal time frame. Increasing your income in line with a budgeting strategy will result in saving a house deposit while the dream of buying a home is still alive.

- Lifestyle creep occurs when your spending increases as your income grows. You need to avoid this to maximise your chances of saving a house deposit.

# 3 | INCREASE your INCOME

With the cost of living at an all-time high, it's become increasingly challenging for average Australians to reduce their essential spending. For many, the only way to save a house deposit in a reasonable time frame would be to increase their income. In chapter 4, we are going to unpack the strategies required to negotiate your salary, apply for a new full-time job and even change industries. But before you go resigning from your current employer, let's first analyse ways to increase your income while keeping your full-time gig. If you feel secure, supported and generally happy in your current job, then why not look at ways to supplement your income rather than replace it?

After working as a high-school maths teacher for 4 years, I found that my annual salary had peaked. This is because I had secured a level 3 teaching position, a role granted to teachers who prove they're working at an exceptional level. They are then paid at the level of a deputy principal in the hopes they stay in the classroom rather than climb up through the ranks of management. At the time, it was a reasonable income. But the decisions my wife and I made in our 20s left us with an astronomically large mortgage. Our combined income of $193 000 wasn't enough to live on and make our home loan repayments.

Remember what I said about lifestyle creep in chapter 2? Well, we were the biggest culprits because we wanted to turn our old, dilapidated 1960 weatherboard house into our dream home and, as we found out the hard way, renovations aren't cheap! The problem with our type of lifestyle creep is that we were constantly spending money throughout the renovation to make our home liveable. As the renovation costs escalated, so did our mortgage repayments—and before we knew it, we were in the red.

We were cornered financially. To continue with our renovations, we had to borrow more money. But the only way we could afford a bigger loan was by increasing our overall income. Since my full-time salary had peaked, I was forced to brainstorm ways to supplement my income. My first solution was simple. I could get a second job working somewhere like Bunnings. I could work a few nights a week or maybe even on weekends. It was a rate of $30 an hour—substantially less than I was earning as a teacher—but beggars can't be choosers. I hit 'submit' on my application that night, but little did I know, the very next day a request from the mother of one of my students asking me to tutor one of her children would completely change my income journey.

## My side hustle

For my first private tutoring session, I was paid $60 for an hour of my time. Not only was this a far better deal than I could find in casual retail, but it was also roughly the same as my teaching rate.

Determined to finish our renovations and take control of our finances, I started brainstorming ways to secure more tutoring clients. It was a great hourly rate, but if I could only secure one hour a week, then I'd be better off taking a pay cut and locking in several hours at Bunnings.

My marketing philosophy was simple: provide a high-quality service, then let everyone know it exists. Before I knew it, my student's mother had referred me to three of her friends. At four students a week, I was making $240 before tax. I felt like my side hustle had legs.

Just as I was running out of ideas for expanding my business, my wife mentioned Facebook groups. I was a social media virgin at the time and had no idea what she was talking about. But, with her help I joined all the local groups, searched for 'tutoring' and commented on every single relevant post from the previous 6 months. I had two goals when commenting:

1. Provide value

2. Let them know I offer tuition services.

After a week of commenting on more than 500 posts, I secured an additional 12 students. At 16 students a week, I was earning $960 a week before tax from my tutoring business. We were taking control of our finances, but now I had another problem. I was working 16 hours a week on top of full-time teaching. At close to 60 hours a week, I was burning the candle at both ends.

Then, one day, during a year 7 maths class, it hit me. In class I regularly asked students to work in groups because it increases their engagement and maximises their achievements. Why not replicate this model with the students I tutored?

I told the parents of my existing students that I was transitioning to a small-group tutoring model of four students. I reduced the cost from $60 to $50 per hour. This meant that, with 16 students, I was earning $800 a week before tax, 17 per cent less than before, but I was only working 4 hours a week (75 per cent less than the single-student tuition model). The success of this transition ignited a spark. If I could grow my side hustle, not only could it give us the financial security we dreamed of, but it might even give me the confidence to go part time as a teacher.

Good word-of-mouth travels fast. By the end of the year, I was back to tutoring 16 hours a week on top of teaching fulltime, but this time servicing 64 students. Before tax, I was earning $3200 a week from my side hustle — almost double my income as a full-time teacher. Financially, we were sorted.

However, I soon came to realise that the time required to run a business of that size far exceeded 16 hours a week. Communicating with parents outside of tutoring hours, tracking payments, scheduling invoices and consistently marketing meant I was working closer to 30 hours a week. Combined with my teaching role, I was working just over 70 hours a week. As my business grew, despite transitioning to a part-time teaching role my work hours peaked at 80 hours a week. After sleeping for 7 hours a night, this only gave me 39 hours out of the 119 hours a week I was awake to enjoy life. I had been blindly chasing financial security for so long that I had ignored the need for a balanced, healthy lifestyle. Instead of feeling financially suffocated, I was feeling completely burnt out.

You might be thinking, 'Robbo, I thought you were going to teach me how to increase my income. Why do you keep referring to how many hours you were working?'

The answer is simple: if you supplement your income with secondary employment or a side hustle, it's likely that you'll start making financial decisions based on that increased overall income. These decisions could lock you into an added workload. So, you need to ask yourself, 'Is this sustainable?'

> **REFLECT**
>
> **Time diary**
>
> Before you make the decision to increase your working hours, it's important to reflect on the time you have available. Do you have any spare time, and if so, are you willing to spend it working to increase your income?
>
> Completing a time diary like the one below based on one standard week will be an eye-opener, I guarantee it. Try writing in the hours you spend doing the various activities.
>
> *(continued)*

| | Number of hours spent | | | | | | | |
|---|---|---|---|---|---|---|---|---|
| | Sleeping | Working | In transit | Exercising | Doing household chores | Caring for children | Undertaking leisure activities | Total |
| Mon | | | | | | | | 24 |
| Tue | | | | | | | | 24 |
| Wed | | | | | | | | 24 |
| Thu | | | | | | | | 24 |
| Fri | | | | | | | | 24 |
| Sat | | | | | | | | 24 |
| Sun | | | | | | | | 24 |
| **Total** | | | | | | | | **168** |

Filling in this time diary should answer two questions:

1. Do you have any spare time? The biggest indicator will be your total number of leisure hours.
2. If you do have any spare time, on what days would it make sense to take on supplementary work? For most full-time employees, this will be the weekend. For many primary caregivers, this might be at night, once the kids are asleep.

# From DINKs to parents

You read in chapter 1 that the most common way couples earn enough money to buy their first home is by combining their incomes. From the bank's perspective, this ticks all the boxes. But what happens when you decide to start a family? Even with parental leave, there's usually a period where your household income is reduced. In some cases, childcare is so expensive that it's not worth the primary caregiver returning to work. I've met countless couples in this exact position, scrambling to cope with the increased cost of living as a household on a single income. The best way to create a safety net around your household income is to build a supplementary income before you start a family. That way, you can dial this supplementary income up or down as you need it.

Unfortunately, this isn't 1985. To own a home in Australia, particularly if you're earning a median full-time salary, you'll be forced out of your comfort zone. What are you willing to sacrifice to take control of your financial journey?

## The income-tax myth

I'm sure you've heard this before: 'Don't get a second job. Most of the income from a second job will be consumed by taxes!'

This is one of the biggest myths in Australia about income tax. It assumes that since you can only claim the tax-free threshold on one source of income, any additional income you earn will seem like it's being taxed at a higher rate. But this is completely false. Let's look at an example.

### CASE STUDY

### Bazza's extra tax

Bazza earns $60 000 a year before tax. In total, he pays $9888 in tax for the year. If he earned an additional $10 000 before tax from his existing employer, for any reason — whether it be overtime, bonuses or commission — he would pay an additional $3000 in tax. If, instead, Bazza secured secondary employment and earned $10 000 before tax through his second job, he would pay the same amount of tax on the $10 000 — that is, $3000.

---

That's how Australia's marginal tax rate system is structured. It may appear you're earning less when you look at your payslips. However, at tax time you'll receive a refund for the difference owing to you. So don't use this tax myth as a scapegoat when deciding if you should supplement your income.

## Overtime vs secondary employment

When supplementing their income, most people opt to work overtime. This scenario usually results in the least amount of friction. If your employer is offering extra hours, it's practical to continue doing the job you're already paid to do. Most people can also tack the overtime hours onto their standard shifts. In addition to this, many employers pay overtime at a higher hourly rate. It's common to pay one and a half times the hourly rate for hours worked on top of full-time hours. For someone earning $30 an hour, this means for every overtime hour worked, they receive $45. Overtime is a great starting point to supplement your income, especially if you have a great relationship with your employer.

Secondary employment usually takes more effort to get started. In most cases you'll need to go through the application process and win the position over other candidates. (In chapter 4, I'll reveal some strategies you can use to help you with the application process.)

Once the position is yours, particularly if you're working in a part-time capacity, you'll be guaranteed a certain number of hours per week. The important element here will be weighing up your hourly rate. How does it compare to your full-time hourly rate and, more importantly, is it significantly less than any overtime opportunities?

Another factor to consider with secondary employment is that it gives you an opportunity to develop a skill set outside of your current employment. The more skills you have at your disposal throughout your career, the more likely it is that you'll secure a higher paying position.

## The path to a $100 000-per-year side hustle

Not long after I started my tutoring side hustle, I became addicted to small-business podcasts. I wanted to learn everything about building a business, everything about maximising my income. One day, I came across a concept created by Kevin Kelly, and popularised by Tim Ferriss, called '1000 true fans' (you can search for it on YouTube). The concept is simple: if you can convince 1000 people to pay you $10 per month for your services, then you've made over $100 000 per year. Prior to learning about this concept, generating an income of $100 000 a year from my side hustle seemed impossible. But convincing 1000 people to pay me $10 a month, while not easy, seemed achievable.

I adopted this concept and altered it to fit within my side hustle. My students' parents had already committed to paying me $50 per week for small-group tutoring classes. After dividing $100 000 into 52 weeks of the year, then dividing that figure by $50 (the fee for attending a group class), I realised that I only needed 39 students to break the $100 000 threshold. In fact, even if I only elected to work during the 40-week school year, I still only needed 50 students to earn $100 000.

Segmenting a large financial target into smaller, achievable goals is a strategy I continue to use today in my business, Trusted Finance. As my experience in small business grew, so too did my financial targets. Marketing expert Seth Godin elaborates on Kevin Kelly's '1000 true fans' concept by adapting it to an annual target of $1 million. Godin demonstrated that this target could be achieved in several ways, as shown in figure 3.1.

1 person can pay you $1 000 000

10 people can pay you $100 000

100 people can pay you $10 000

1000 people can pay you $1000

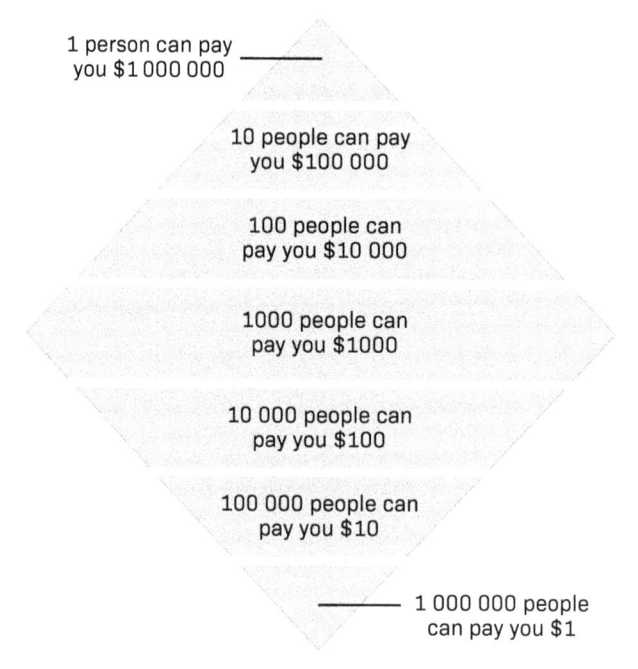

10 000 people can pay you $100

100 000 people can pay you $10

1 000 000 people can pay you $1

**Figure 3.1: ways to achieve an annual income of $1 million**

My journey to creating a seven-figure business is a story for another book, but I want you to understand what's possible if you start a side hustle. If you can figure out a way to provide a service to enough people, your side hustle could grow into a business far bigger than you ever anticipated. There's only one way to guarantee that your side hustle isn't successful: never starting one.

> ### EXPLORE YOUR OPTIONS
>
> ## Supplementing your income
>
> You can use the following formula to calculate how many hours per week you need to work in your side hustle to achieve your savings target. I've given you an example based on someone with a pre-tax income of $80 000 per year from their full-time job.
>
> Annual savings target amount: *$24 000*
>
> Current annual after-tax income (calculate after-tax income at *paycalculator.com.au*): *$63 612*
>
> Combined annual after-tax income and annual savings target: *$24 000 + $63 612 = $87 612*
>
> Total pre-tax income required to earn $87 612 after tax (calculate after-tax income at *paycalculator.com.au*): *$115 300*
>
> Annual side-hustle pre-tax income required (total pre-tax income minus current annual pre-tax income): *$115 300 − $80 000 = $35 300*
>
> Weekly hours of work required based on *$30* an hour (pre-tax side-hustle income ÷ 52 ÷ $30): *$35 300 ÷ 52 ÷ $30 = 22.63*
>
> Number of extra hours I need to work per week to save over $24 000 in one year earning $30 per hour: *23 hours*

Obviously, the more you can earn per hour, the fewer hours you'll need to work to save for a house deposit. But don't let this stop you from starting to increase your income with a side hustle. To start with, you might only earn $25 an hour from your side hustle. But over time, a new full-time job might become available offering a higher hourly rate, or your small business might evolve to generate a larger return for your time.

As I've said before, the point is that you need to act *now*. If you don't currently earn enough money, then you need to start supplementing your income now so that you have enough time to save a house deposit before home ownership becomes completely out of reach.

### CASE STUDY

## Jamal's home-buying journey

Jamal decided he wanted to buy a home by the time he was 26. Back in 2022, he secured a job as a full-time insurance adviser, earning $87 000 per year before tax. After running his income through a maximum borrowing calculator online he realised his income wasn't going to be enough to buy a house. Jamal decided to start a side hustle. He posted on his neighbourhood's Facebook group that he was willing to clean out anyone's gutters for $150.

Thirty minutes after posting, he booked his first client. The job took 4 hours on a Saturday, but it put him $150 closer to his house deposit savings target. After a few weeks of consistently booking one gutter clean every Saturday, Jamal cut the average job time in half to only 2 hours. Allowing 30 minutes between each job, he calculated that he could easily do three gutter cleans every Saturday. He spent his lunch breaks during the week advertising his services in other Facebook groups and booked himself months in advance. His side hustle consistently generated $450 a week, or just over $23 000 a year. He saved all the after-tax income generated from his side hustle, which came to $39 780 over two and a half years. Initially, Jamal's goal was to buy an existing house, but in 2024, the Queensland Government announced a $30 000 First Home Owner Grant (FHOG) for anyone choosing to build their first home.

## Jamal's financial snapshot

| | | | |
|---|---|---|---|
| Annual before-tax income | $87 000 fulltime $23 400 side hustle | Monthly living expenses | $2300 |
| Job title | Insurance adviser Business owner | Total credit card limits | $2000 |
| Total savings | $39 780 | Monthly personal loan repayments | $0 |
| Eligible for government support | Yes: FHOG, FHBG and stamp duty exemption | Monthly student debt repayments | $0 |
| Parent guarantor | No | Residency status | Australian citizen |

## Jamal's outcome

Since Jamal had been operating his gutter cleaning business for more than 2 years, he was able to include it in his home loan calculation. With a maximum borrowing power of $540 000, Jamal elected to buy a block of land for $290 000 and build a four-bedroom, two-bathroom

*(continued)*

house for $310 000. Since he bought a block of land priced at under Queensland's stamp duty exemption threshold (see the tables in chapter 6 for the thresholds applicable to each state and territory) as a first home buyer he avoided paying property tax. He also secured a spot in the FHBG (I explain FHBG, FHOG and LMI in chapter 6), meaning he only needed to contribute a 5 per cent deposit and wasn't charged LMI by his bank. Jamal also claimed the $30 000 FHOG, resulting in a home loan of $535 000 against a property worth $600 000. While Jamal's property is being constructed, he is only paying interest on the land portion of his home loan. As the builder is funded each progress payment, Jamal's minimum interest repayments will go up. Eventually, Jamal's principal and interest repayments will be $781 per week.

# Key takeaways
# for your home-buying journey

- You can increase your overall income by working a second job or starting your own business. These are known as side hustles.

- Since these side hustles are usually worked in addition to full-time employment, they can drastically increase your overall work hours.

- Once you have adjusted to a new level of increased income, it's likely you will make financial decisions that lock you into this increased income so you must determine if the extra workload is sustainable.

- For couples, supplementing one person's income can help ease the burden of starting a family. If one of you can adopt the role of primary caregiver, you'll save money by not paying for day care.

- The concept that your secondary employment is taxed at a higher rate is a myth due to Australia's marginal tax rate system.

- Overtime is a great way to increase your income if you're satisfied with your current employer as it usually pays an increased hourly rate. Working a second job can give you the opportunity to develop new skills, while also earning an income, which could be utilised throughout your career to secure higher paying full-time roles.

- Kevin Kelly explains that if you can convince 1000 people to pay you $10 a month, then in a year, you'll have made over $100 000. How can you apply this idea to your own side hustle?

# 4 | What are YOU WORTH?

In this chapter you're going to figure out what you're worth. What's the best hourly rate you can achieve right now? What about in a year from now? Focusing on your hourly rate will maximise your income and minimise your working time.

You can begin by negotiating a better salary with your existing employer. Or, if they don't play ball, it might be time to jump ship.

This is where your resume comes in. To maximise your chances of securing a promotion or being offered a new job, you need to structure your resume the right way.

## The moment I realised my own worth

When I was 19 years old, I dreamed of travelling around the world. I vowed to myself that I would make it happen by the time I was 21. There was one problem. A 4-month round-the-world trip was expensive and as a full-time university student working casually at Coles in the fruit and veg department, I was earning just enough each week to buy five beers and a kebab down at the Curtin University tavern. I calculated that I needed to save around $40 000. On my Coles wage of $17 an hour, working roughly 20 hours a week, it would take 118 weeks—or 2 years and 14 weeks—to save enough. For a moment I considered it. I was still living with my parents, and since I was studying fulltime, they weren't charging me any rent. But then I remembered petrol, my phone bill and all the things I'd need to spend money on over the next 2 years to retain at least one ounce of sanity. Something had to change.

I was so fixated on saving $40 000 that I was willing to work anywhere. I started by dropping off my resume at different stores and cafes in the shopping centre closest to my home. But after going to a few interviews, I realised they all paid roughly the same hourly rate as Coles. Minimum wage. I needed to be more strategic. I needed to do some research. Up until that point I had been applying for anything, burning my time interviewing for a position without knowing if the job was going to get me any closer to my $40 000 savings target. That was when I realised I could search more specifically online using websites like *Seek*.

If you're thinking, 'Robbo, did it really take you this long to consider using *Seek*?', remember that it was 2007, I was 19 years old and I still used a Nokia 3315. Smartphones had only just been invented and I definitely didn't have the cash to buy one. In fact, I didn't even have a laptop. I was using my parents' desktop computer. But that was good enough for searching for jobs, filtering them based on income level.

First, I searched for jobs that earned the most per hour. I quickly realised that they all required some sort of qualification. I remember reading through hundreds of job descriptions—from lawyers to project managers to engineers—thinking that one day that would be me. But for now, I needed to figure out how much I could earn with no formal qualifications.

I had proven customer service experience... and that was about it! As I filtered through lower hourly rates, I started to see a trend. Companies that operated during traditional business hours—Monday to Friday from 9 am until 5 pm—were offering incentives to potential employees willing to work outside of these hours. Maybe I could work when all their full-time employees refused to.

I just needed to find a job category that didn't require any qualifications. Something that a range of industries needed. Then it dawned on me. Sales! After narrowing my search, I found an advertised position working for a flight-booking centre. A higher hourly rate than I was on and a commission on the sales I made. Feeling very smug, I hit the submit button. Now all I needed to do was wait...

A couple of weeks went by and I didn't hear anything. With my tail between my legs, I contacted the recruitment manager.

'Unfortunately, you didn't make it past the first stage review of your resume.'

Getting a new job was turning out to be harder than I first thought. Back to *seek* to find a different opportunity. On the second attempt, I applied to an insurance company. It gave me the same result. I didn't even make it past the first stage. But this time I did something different. When I called the recruitment manager, I asked her why my resume wasn't selected. She said, 'You have no sales experience, and you haven't given any examples of your communication or negotiation skills'.

She was right. Since the age of 14, the only place I had worked was Coles. This left me completely deflated. How on earth was I going to get my first job in sales if I needed sales experience to begin with? I stopped searching for jobs. I started to reconsider my savings target. Maybe $40 000 was completely unachievable for someone with my skill set. *Maybe I'll just need to save for longer or go on a shorter trip.*

Then one day, while I was chopping and wrapping watermelons at Coles, I overheard my fruit and veg manager arguing with a supplier over the price of strawberries. After he hung up the phone in a complete rage, I asked him about the call. He said that negotiating with suppliers was the worst part of his job. My mind was running a million miles an hour and out of nowhere I said, 'I can help you with those calls'.

He raised an eyebrow.

'If you train me to talk to the suppliers, I can do it for you.'

He was sceptical, but he disliked doing it so much that he agreed. Before I knew it, I was communicating with suppliers on most shifts. I was negotiating on quantities, price and delivery schedules. Finally, I had some ammunition.

Time to go job hunting again. This time I came across a sales position working for a large bank located in the CBD. Before hitting the submit button I asked myself a simple question: 'How can I prove to the recruitment manager reading my resume that I actually have the skills they require?'

I started by listing everything I had learned while speaking to suppliers at Coles:

- I negotiate with suppliers on best price.
- I listen to their concerns and, by working with my manager, come up with solutions to their problems.
- I communicate the delivery schedules of products to different teams within the business.
- I have been given authority to make decisions independently while communicating with suppliers in the best interest of the business.

In addition to the above, which may have been slightly exaggerated, I described how I approach all tasks with enthusiasm and dedication. Finally, I elaborated on my relationship with my own finances, describing how I've spent time researching the best savings accounts to maximise the return on my own money.

That moment when I made the decision to step up while cutting watermelon had paid off. I was offered an interview at a bank 2 weeks later and emailed several topics to help me prepare. I was so nervous. All I needed to do was prove that I had the skills I described in my resume. I came prepared with five examples of how I communicate, negotiate, collaborate and take on new responsibilities at Coles. A few days later I was formally offered the part-time position, working 20 hours from Monday to Friday. I was ecstatic as my hourly rate increased from $17 to $25, but more importantly they were desperate for their staff to volunteer for weekend shifts.

After I had finished my onboard training, I jumped at the opportunity to work weekends. I assumed the bank would pay time and a half, equalling $37.50 an hour, but I was wrong. The weekend rate was *double time and a half*. For every hour I worked on the weekend, I was earning $62.50. I couldn't believe it. That was almost a 4-hour shift at Coles. To maximise the amount I was earning each week, I elected to work an 8-hour shift on Saturdays and Sundays. In total, I was working 20 hours from Monday to Friday, plus 16 hours over the weekend, on top of my full-time university timetable. But due to the weekend overtime, I was getting paid for 60 standard hours even though I was only working 36 hours.

In less than 2 years I hit my savings target. I graduated university with more than $40 000 in the bank and spent 4 months travelling the world with one of my best mates. The trip was everything I had wanted it to be and more. And now, looking back on that part of my life, I realise the problem-solving skills I developed to save the $40 000 built an incredibly valuable foundation. I learned how to search for new opportunities, how to make myself look desirable in the eyes of an employer and, most importantly, I learned what I was worth. I learned that my worth was limitless.

## REFLECT

### Your current situation

This chapter is designed to teach you how to increase your income over time through salary negotiations or by taking advantage of new employment opportunities. But before I teach you how to maximise your income, you need to reflect on your current situation.

Consider the following when reflecting on where you're at right now:

- Job title
- Annual income before tax
- Weekly income before tax (annual income ÷ 52)
- Hourly income (weekly income ÷ hours worked)
- Do you have an option for overtime?
- If so, what is the hourly rate and is the overtime consistent?
- Weekly travel time to and from work
- How many weeks of annual paid leave do you receive?
- Does your employer offer other added benefits (company car, mobile, laptop)?
- Key responsibilities at your current job (list at least 5).
- Does your job make you happy? Why / Why not?

# Setting your income goals

Now that you've reflected on your current situation, it's time to set your income goals. Working in a career without an income goal is like trying to hit a bullseye with a bow and arrow blindfolded. You'll show up every single day with bow in hand, ready to work, and spend 99 per cent of your time shooting without getting anywhere close to the bullseye. In fact, you're blindfolded, so you wouldn't even know if you hit the target in the first place! The point that I'm trying to make, is that you have a much higher likelihood of making decisions in the moment that steer you towards your desired income if you can define exactly how much you need to earn to have the lifestyle you deserve.

In chapter 1, you did some research. You analysed the current property market across three Australian cities and determined approximately what you could buy on your current income. You then searched for more desirable properties that would cost more than you could afford at this time. Keep these tasks in mind as you complete the following income goals section.

When setting any type of goal, it's important to follow the SMART goals framework made popular by George T Doran in the early 1980s. The acronym 'SMART' prompts the user to create a goal with a high likelihood of success, as opposed to pulling a target out of thin air. SMART stands for:

- **S** – *Specific.* Target a specific area of improvement.
- **M** – *Measurable.* Can you measure whether you've achieved your target?
- **A** – *Achievable, Accountable, Assignable.* Can it be done? If so, who's going to do it?

- **R** – *Relevant.* How is this goal relevant to your other life goals?

- **T** – *Timebound.* When can the results be achieved?

You can use the SMART framework to create your income goal by answering the questions in table 4.1.

**Table 4.1: creating an income goal using the SMART framework**

| Specific | How much do you want to earn per year before tax? |
|---|---|
| Measurable | What are the maximum number of hours per week you are willing to work to achieve this target? Therefore, what is your hourly rate target? |
| Achievable, accountable, assignable | Do employers actually pay the salary you are chasing? Do you think you will need to change industries? What research have you done to support your answers to these two questions? |
| Relevant | Using the website *paycalculator* determine your weekly after-tax income. What will this income do for your lifestyle? Where and what type of home could you buy on this income? |
| Timebound | How long will it take you to achieve this new income level? Are you expecting to jump from your current income straight to your desired income or will you achieve this in smaller increments? |

## Negotiating your salary

If you're happy in your current job, you can work towards your income goal by negotiating your salary with your current employer. The FY23/24 Hayes Salary Guide reported that only

28 per cent of Australian employees are happy with their salary. However, 35 per cent are not confident enough to ask for a raise.

To earn an above-average salary, you need to be willing to negotiate with your employer, even if that means engaging in an uncomfortable conversation. But where do you start? The mistake most employees make is that they expect to be able to simply approach their boss and ask for a raise. In the first instance they're usually rejected, and then they give up. But it's called a negotiation for a reason. To maximise the likelihood your employer will negotiate, follow these six steps.

## 1. What are your expectations and your limits?

When entering a negotiation with your employer it's important to have two numbers in mind. One that represents your desired pay increase and one that represents the minimum pay increase you'll accept. Before you enter this discussion, you need to do your research. Are there other employers offering a more competitive salary for a similar role? Are any of your colleagues earning more than you for doing a similar job? Do your current responsibilities fall outside of others doing a similar job to yours?

## 2. What are your employer's goals?

During a negotiation, it's important to understand your employer's expectations of you as an employee. If your current role has key performance indicators (KPIs), then this will form a solid foundation for discussing your employer's expectations. If your role doesn't have a measurable performance indicator, then your goal in this discussion should be to agree upon how your key responsibilities are measured. You can then ask what your employer requires for you to achieve the desired salary increase. If this conversation is embedded into your standard performance review, you can use your performance feedback as ammunition to justify your desired salary increase. If you don't receive consistent performance reviews, then this is your opportunity to ask for feedback. But make sure your employer gives you a clear, measurable set of KPIs to reach so that you can justify a salary increase once you've achieved them.

### 3. How will your new salary impact your employer?

It's important to highlight the benefits for your employer of your new salary. Your employer will be paying you more, so what are they getting out of it? Are you currently taking on leadership responsibilities without the commensurate income? Or, are you willing to take on more responsibilities within the business to justify your desired salary? Understanding your employer's goals will give you the insight required to customise your job description just enough to justify an increase in pay.

### 4. What other benefits can your employer offer?

While your goal is to increase your income, a starting point that might be more digestible for your employer could be added employee benefits. These benefits could include paid time off, work schedule or location flexibility, paid-for training opportunities or paid health insurance. Asking to include related training could enhance your employer's perception of your commitment to their business, increasing the likelihood they will meet your income goals into the future.

## 5. When is the right time to ask?

The most common time a salary negotiation occurs is at the time of an employee milestone such as a one-year anniversary of service. It might also make sense to raise this discussion after successfully meeting a deadline or receiving positive feedback from your employer. But the earlier you plant this seed, the more time you will have to watch it grow. Make your employer aware as soon as you can that you want to help them grow their business to a new level, but you also want to be paid accordingly.

## 6. Are you prepared to negotiate?

If you've never negotiated your salary before, then don't expect to get what you want in the first meeting. Your manager or employer will most likely be an experienced salary negotiator. So, it's important that you're prepared to play the long game. Every time you negotiate, you'll get better at it. Moving forward, it's important to remain confident in your professional abilities and stay updated with changing salaries in your industry to ensure you're prepared for your next meeting.

Starting the conversation is often the scariest part. If you're stuck on what to say, Open Universities Australia identified a few things to mention for your first meeting:

- Provide clear examples of your achievements.

- Be enthusiastic for future work.

- Show you're underpaid by providing market research around skills and salary.

- Propose a new salary based on the industry standard.

### 🏠 EXPLORE YOUR OPTIONS

## Finding a job that pays your desired income

Most Australians don't update their resume regularly. In fact, it's not until they're faced with losing their job or they want to secure a new job opportunity that they are prompted to review it. When they update it, most fall into the same trap. They update it with all the responsibilities they've ever had and list all of the results they've ever achieved. Remember, when you try to write your resume to everyone, you end up writing it to no-one.

But before you refine your resume, you need to do some research.

If you're looking to change jobs, the checklist below is a good starting point for preparing your resume. Begin by searching for jobs in your preferred industry that pay your desired income. As you saw earlier, I like to use *Seek*. If you're unable to obtain all of the information from the job advertisement, call the employer's contact, which should be listed in the advertisement, for further clarification.

☐ Name of employer

☐ Job title

*(continued)*

- ☐ Advertised salary
- ☐ Does this salary match your income goal?
- ☐ If not, how far from your goal is it?
- ☐ What are the essential qualifications and skills required?
- ☐ What are the desirable qualifications and skills required?
- ☐ What are the key responsibilities?
- ☐ Are you able to apply for this job now? If not, what qualifications or skills do you need to obtain before you're ready?

## Refine your resume

Now that you've done some research, select your referred job. It's time to get out your resume and start refining it based on this job's essential qualifications or skills, desirable qualifications or skills, and key responsibilities. Some advertised positions also require you to complete selection criteria. These criteria will need to be completed in addition to your resume. Other positions will ask for a cover letter in addition to your resume. The selection criteria or cover letter give you the opportunity to showcase your qualifications and skills using examples. The resume provides a summary of your previous roles, key responsibilities, the year you completed your qualifications and reference contact information.

The cover letter or selection criteria can be written in a variety of formats. One way is to use the Situation, Action, Outcome

(SAO) structure I introduced in chapter 1. The trick here is to find four or five strong examples of how you have achieved outcomes in a previous role that mirror what the advertising employer wants you to achieve for their business. You need to prove to them that you are the perfect candidate for the position. In other words, you need to sell yourself.

Back in chapter 1 you reflected on nine SAOs that demonstrated the key attributes employers look for in an employee. You can use these as a starting point, but it's important to make your SAOs very specific to your chosen job. First, describe a situation or problem you experienced in your current or a previous workplace that your potential employer might experience. These situations are usually problems faced by the business. Then you need to describe the actions you took to solve the problem:

- Why did you implement these strategies?

- How did you collaborate with your colleagues to solve this problem?

- Did you take on a leadership role?

- What did this leadership role look like?

- How was communication managed throughout this journey?

Finally, what was the outcome of your actions? It's important to describe the positive impact you had on your current employer's business goals. Your new employer will want to be sure that you're invested in growing their company.

For each job you apply for, you should create a job-specific SAO. You can use the following structure in your resume:

*Name of employer and job title:*
*Which essential or desirable skill is your SAO linked to?*
*Situation:*
*Action:*
*Outcome:*

• • •

Actively searching for new employment opportunities, understanding the importance of salary negotiation and putting the steps in place to be paid what you're worth are integral elements to earning an above-average income. The income goal you've established in this chapter hasn't been pulled out of thin air. It's based on the current state of the property market in Australia and on the amount you need to earn to create the life you deserve. The sooner you commit to refining your resume in line with future opportunities, the sooner you'll reach your income goal. Don't be afraid to start the conversation or apply for a new position. The worst thing they can do is say no.

## CASE STUDY

## Daniel and Emma's home-buying journey

Daniel and Emma met in 2015 while on a Contiki tour in Europe. After a year of trying to make a long-distance relationship work, Emma packed her bags and left Perth to live with Daniel in New Zealand. Seven years and two children later, Daniel and Emma, now aged 38 and 35 respectively, decided to move to Perth to be closer to her family. Before they committed to the move, Daniel secured a job working FIFO in a processing position. Daniel, Emma and their two children moved in with Emma's parents while they transitioned to their new life in Perth. Once they started looking for a rental it became clear that it was going to be much harder than they thought. In Perth, at the time, the rental vacancy rate was below 0.4 per cent, making it highly competitive to secure a rental property. They started to consider if it might be easier to buy a home instead. With Daniel working FIFO, they were receiving a great income, but the move to Perth drained their bank account. With less than $3000 in savings, it was impossible to secure a home loan.

## *Daniel and Emma's financial snapshot*

| | | | |
|---|---|---|---|
| Daniel's annual before-tax income | $176 000 | Parent guarantor | Yes |
| Emma's annual before-tax income | $0 | Monthly living expenses | $3500 |
| Total annual before-tax income | $176 000 | Total credit card limits | $10 000 |
| Job titles | Daniel: FIFO operator Emma: Stay-at-home mum | Monthly personal loan repayments | $0 |
| Total savings | $3000 | Monthly student debt repayments | $0 |

*(continued)*

| **Eligible for government support** | No: property price is above WA thresholds for all government benefits | **Residency status** | Daniel: New Zealand citizen Emma: Australian citizen |

## Daniel and Emma's outcome

Emma's parents had bought their home in 2006. They have less than $200 000 owing on their home loan. After realising how hard it was for Emma and Daniel to secure a rental property, they offered to become their guarantors. Their home is worth $900 000, meaning they have just over $700 000 in equity.

Daniel and Emma's maximum borrowing power equates to $648 000. But, since Daniel and Emma have very little in savings, Emma's parents would need to secure 20 per cent of the purchased property as well as all the upfront costs against their home. This would leave Daniel and Emma with a mortgage above the value of the home they purchased.

They set their budget at $600 000 (which was deliberately lower than their borrowing power) and fell in love with a three-bedroom, two-bathroom house. Their offer of $610 000 was accepted, resulting in a mortgage of $636 000. The repayments on their home loan are $928 per week, substantially more than they would have paid in rent, but now they'll own their own home before they reach retirement.

# Key takeaways for your home-buying journey

- The challenge is to increase your hourly rate so the number of hours you work each week is sustainable. When you buy a home, you're committing to a 30-year mortgage. Can you continue working this many hours per week for 30 years?

- You can increase the likelihood of achieving a goal by using the SMART framework. Make sure your goal is Specific, Measurable, Achievable/Accountable/Assignable, Relevant and Timebound.

- Ask yourself the following questions when entering a salary negotiation with your employer:

    - What are your expectations and your limits?

    - What are your employer's goals?

    - How will your salary impact your employer?

    - What other benefits can your employer offer?

    - When is the right time to ask for a salary review?

    - Are you prepared to negotiate?

- When you're applying for a new job, it's important to update your resume in line with the advertised position. You can use the SAO format (Situation, Action, Outcome) to showcase your abilities, making sure to link your example to the advertised position's essential or desirable skills.

# PART II
# BUY *your* FIRST HOME

# 5 | How much CAN YOU BORROW?

There are two main roadblocks to buying a house in Australia. The first is how much you need in savings to pay for the deposit and upfront costs. (In chapter 6, I'll teach you how to minimise the savings required to enter the housing market.) The second is how much the bank will let you borrow for a home loan. It's important to understand what factors will reduce your maximum borrowing power so you can make informed financial decisions in the lead-up to buying your first home.

Recently, I met a first home buyer named Aaron. He was furious that his maximum borrowing power was only $350 000 when his co-worker with an identical income was able to borrow $550 000.

Aaron's problem was that he was focused on how much they earned, rather than how each of them spent their money. The difference in their monthly living expenses and overall liabilities equated to a $200 000 difference in home loan lending capacity.

So how can you ensure your borrowing power is at its peak when you apply for a home loan?

# Income vs expenses and liabilities

Banks determine your maximum borrowing power using a rather simple equation. They input your after-tax income, then deduct your living expenses and repayments made towards your liabilities. This surplus is then used to determine the maximum monthly payments you could make towards a mortgage. The bank will allocate a 'buffer' to maximise the likelihood that you could make increased repayments in case interest rates rise. This repayment figure is then used to determine your maximum borrowing power.

Each bank follows its own set of lending guidelines to create its home-loan products, to determine your minimum deposit required and calculate your borrowing power. This is why one bank might calculate your borrowing power as slightly higher than another bank. As a home buyer, it can be overwhelming and time consuming to figure out which bank will offer you the highest borrowing power. As someone who has bought properties directly through a bank as well as through a mortgage broker, I can safely say that the mortgage broker route has saved me the most time and provided me with the best home loan product. This is why mortgage brokers are now responsible for organising over 70 per cent of home loans administered in Australia each year.

When you're ready to take your first steps towards home ownership, my network of mortgage brokers will be able to support you through the journey completely free of charge. In the meantime, use the information in this chapter to correctly structure your finances in the eyes of the bank.

# Living expenses

Banks adopt a range of methods to calculate your living expenses, according to their lending guidelines. The method they use can have a massive impact on your maximum borrowing power.

- *Method 1:* As discussed in chapter 2, most banks use the household expenditure measure (HEM) — which is based on your family size, location and income — to determine your living expenses. The banks justify using this as the reasonable minimum for your living expenses because the data to create the HEM is sourced from the Australian Bureau of Statistics (ABS). If you're someone who lives well below their means, then a bank using the HEM guidelines (as opposed to using your actual living expenses) could reduce your borrowing power far below what you could afford.

- *Method 2:* Your bank might ask you to self-assess your living expenses. They will then review all your bank accounts and credit cards to verify your self-assessment. Banks are able to access 'one touch' software to download your bank statements for the prior 6 months. So, when self-assessing, it's important to report a realistic figure. Banks using this method will often adjust your living expenses to reflect your last 6 months of spending, so it's imperative to reduce the number of spending blowouts you have in the lead-up to applying for a home loan.

- *Method 3:* Your bank might get you to self-assess, review all your accounts and calculate your living expenses using the HEM method.

Some banks use a combination of the above methods, and then use the biggest living expenses figure in their borrowing power calculations. To put this into perspective, someone earning $100 000 per year before taxes, borrowing at a 6.3 per cent per year interest rate, with living expenses of $1800 per month could borrow approximately $540 000. With living expenses of $2500 per month, this drops to $469 000 and at $3200 per month it reduces to $384 000.

## Liabilities

Liabilities are classified as outstanding debts that require ongoing repayments. The most common types of liabilities in Australia are personal loans, credit cards, Buy Now Pay Later debt and student loans. Each of these debts impacts your borrowing power in different ways, but as a rule of thumb, the more debt you have, the less you'll be able to borrow for a home loan.

### *Personal loans*

There are two main types of personal loans in Australia: secured loans and unsecured loans. A secured personal loan is a loan guaranteed by an asset such as a car. This becomes security for the bank so that if you stop repaying your loan the bank can sell the car to cover its costs. An unsecured personal loan is one for which you don't have to provide security. You can use an unsecured personal loan to fund a holiday or renovate your home, for example. Unsecured personal loans generally attract a higher interest rate as they are a riskier investment for the bank.

The size of the personal loan, the loan term and the interest rate are used to calculate your minimum repayments. The minimum repayment is the figure used by your bank when calculating your maximum home loan borrowing power. Table 5.1 outlines the repayment differences between a secured and an unsecured personal loan of $30 000.

**Table 5.1: difference in repayments between a secured and an unsecured personal loan**

| Loan size of $30 000 | Monthly repayments for 3-year loan term | Monthly repayments for 5-year loan term | Monthly repayments for 7-year loan term |
| --- | --- | --- | --- |
| Secured personal loan at 10% p.a. | $969 | $638 | $499 |
| Unsecured personal loan at 17% p.a. | $1070 | $746 | $614 |

The higher the repayment, the more your personal loan will reduce your maximum home loan borrowing power. Let's look at the impact these personal loans would have on a single applicant's borrowing power if they are living a moderate lifestyle and earning $100 000 per year. See table 5.2 (overleaf) for details.

Table 5.2: impact of a personal loan on a single applicant's borrowing power

| Loan size of $30 000 | 3-year personal loan term reduction in home loan borrowing power | 5-year personal loan term reduction in home loan borrowing power | 7-year personal loan term reduction in home loan borrowing power |
|---|---|---|---|
| Secured personal loan at 10% p.a. | $117 000 | $77 000 | $50 000 |
| Unsecured personal loan at 17% p.a. | $129 000 | $90 000 | $74 000 |

You can see from table 5.2 that, for example, a 3-year secured personal loan at 10 per cent per year would reduce the borrowing power of a single applicant living a moderate lifestyle and earning $100 000 per year by $117 000.

Personal loans, in particular car loans, are the most common type of debt blocking people from buying their first home. Many people get a car loan without realising the negative impact it can have on their home buying journey. The reduction in borrowing power can price you out of your desired suburb or alter the type of dwelling you can afford. I've worked with home buyers who are forced to buy an apartment instead of a house because their car loan has reduced their maximum borrowing power so much that there isn't a house in their price range within a 90-minute drive from the CBD.

To put it bluntly, you don't need to buy an expensive car. In fact, you don't need to take out a personal loan to buy a car. If you're serious about buying a home, you'll find an affordable car that you can buy in cash. My second-hand, 2007 Toyota Camry was $12 000 when I bought it in 2013. As I write this, in June of 2024, I still drive this car every day. Any reason you might be using to justify a more expensive car purchase is probably bullshit. In the long line of sacrifices you'll need to make to buy your first home, this is one of them.

## Credit cards

Credit cards are basically a personal loan that you can tap into at any time. The maximum you can borrow is known as your 'credit card limit'. Most people would correctly assume that an outstanding credit card debt would negatively impact their home loan borrowing power. What they don't anticipate is that a bank will calculate your maximum home loan borrowing power using your credit card *limit*, not your outstanding balance. This is because, at any point after securing your home loan, you could borrow up to the limit of your credit card, forcing you to make the maximum credit card repayments, which could potentially affect your ability to make your home loan repayments.

When you apply for a home loan, it's common for a bank to approve your application pending either the reduction or the cancellation of your credit card. If you have nothing outstanding on your credit card, this is an easy requirement to meet. If you have a sizeable debt on your credit card, then you might be forced to use a portion of savings you've already allocated towards your house deposit to pay off the card. Securing a mortgage is about maximising your borrowing power while preserving your savings to be used for a house deposit and upfront costs. Let's investigate the impact a credit card of various limits will have on the borrowing power of a single applicant living a moderate lifestyle and earning $100 000 per year (see table 5.3).

**Table 5.3: impact of a credit card with various limits on a single applicant's borrowing power**

|  | Credit card limit of $1000 | Credit card limit of $10 000 | Credit card limit of $30 000 |
| --- | --- | --- | --- |
| **Reduction in home loan borrowing power** | $4000 | $43 000 | $135 000 |

## *Buy Now Pay Later (BNPL) debt*

Buy Now Pay Later (BNPL) debts are not a recognised credit provider and some companies therefore advertise that these debts don't impact your maximum home loan borrowing power. However, banks will scrutinise your living expenses and financial obligations by analysing your transaction-account and credit-card statements to determine your maximum borrowing power. Since your BNPL debts are automatically deducted from your accounts, a digital footprint of your spending habits will be clearly visible. Consistent or multiple purchases made using BNPL services can indicate that you were short on cash to meet your living expenses, that your lifestyle choices have become reliant on BNPL services or that you have been, or currently are, facing financial hardship.

In saying that, not all use of BNPL services will indicate a risk to the bank. It's important to not overuse the service, pay all debts off on time and make it clear in your spending history that you don't need BNPL services to meet the cost of your living expenses.

## Student loans

You probably didn't realise when you were enrolling at university that your student debt would substantially decrease your maximum home loan borrowing power. The most common type of student debt is the cost incurred by attending university. This can also include debts incurred by completing Vocational Education and Training (VET) courses. In Australia, the government pays the university upfront. The student then incurs a student debt. This used to be known as a Higher Education Contribution Scheme (HECS) debt. It's now called the Higher Education Loan Program (HELP).

Unlike other loans, which force you to make repayments on the debt the moment you spend the funds, a HELP debt allows students to defer repayments until their taxable income reaches a certain level. The more money you earn, the larger the percentage of your income you need to pay towards your HELP debt. Since your income — rather than your outstanding HELP debt — defines your repayments, the higher your income is, the more of an influence your HELP debt will have on the reduction in your maximum home loan borrowing power. You can find the up-to-date HELP repayments thresholds on the ATO's website: search for 'Study and training loan repayment thresholds and rates'.

To determine the impact a HELP debt can have on your maximum home loan borrowing power, let's take a look at two co-workers, Brodie and Ryan (see table 5.4). Brodie has a total HELP debt of $85 000 after completing two undergraduate degrees, whereas Ryan only has a HELP debt of $20 000.

Table 5.4: impact of a HELP debt on maximum borrowing power

|  | Total HELP debt | Annual income before taxes | Min. annual repayment to HELP debt | Total reduction in max. borrowing power |
|---|---|---|---|---|
| **Brodie** | $85 000 | $100 000 | $6000 | $50 000 |
| **Ryan** | $20 000 | $100 000 | $6000 | $50 000 |

You can see in table 5.4 that both Ryan and Brodie are impacted in the same way, regardless of the size of their HELP debt. (And as you saw in table 1.1, there's a significant reduction in maximum borrowing power between someone on a salary of $94 000 and someone on $100 000.) The only benefit of a smaller HELP debt is that it requires less in savings to completely pay it off and increase your maximum borrowing power if needed.

# Interest rates

Home loan interest rates vary at the banks' discretion. In general, as the Reserve Bank of Australia cash rate either increases or decreases, so do home loan interest rates. The lower the interest rate, the smaller the repayment. The smaller the repayment, the more the bank will let you borrow for a home loan. Table 5.5 outlines the impact different interest rates can have on the maximum borrowing power of a single applicant living a moderate lifestyle and earning $100 000 per year.

Table 5.5: impact of various interest rates on your maximum borrowing power

|  | Variable interest rate of 2.5% p.a. | Variable interest rate of 4.5% p.a. | Variable interest rate of 6.5% p.a. |
| --- | --- | --- | --- |
| Maximum borrowing power of a single income applicant earning $100 000 per year | $735 000 | $597 000 | $495 000 |

So, if you can borrow more when interest rates are lower, does that mean you should wait until the interest rate is optimal? I wish I had a crystal ball and could tell you exactly when to buy your first home. What I can say is that it's easier to predict what will happen in the long term than in the short term. For example, if property values rise during the time you're waiting for interest rates to drop, then even though your borrowing power has increased, you might end up buying the same standard of property but with a bigger mortgage.

# Debt stacking

You may be in a position where your borrowing power is so heavily impacted by your liabilities that you're unable to borrow enough for a home loan to buy even the cheapest apartment in your city. In this case, it's important to pay off your liabilities in order to increase your borrowing power. Debt stacking is a strategy whereby you pay off your highest interest debts first, followed by your lower interest debts, by making the same monthly repayments. It works by following these steps:

1. Stack your debts in order from highest interest rate to lowest interest rate.

2. Calculate the combined minimum monthly repayments for all debts.

3. Can you contribute any extra towards these debts from your income each month? If so, pay these extra funds onto the highest interest debt in your stack.

### REFLECT

## Create your debt stack

If you have liabilities, complete a table like the one below to ascertain your debt stack and to begin paying off those debts. Start by identifying the debt with the highest interest rate. List these debts in descending interest rate order.

| Debt type | Total outstanding | Annual interest rate | Min. monthly repayment | Extra monthly contribution |
|---|---|---|---|---|
| Credit card | $4300 | 19.8% | $86 | $900 |
| Car loan | $21 000 | 12.1% | $372 | |
| Total min. monthly repayments | | | | $458 |
| Total min. monthly repayments + extra monthly contribution | | | | $1358 |

4. Once the highest interest debt is paid off, continue paying the same total each month towards your debts. The next highest interest debt in your stack should be getting paid off at a faster rate because it's receiving the minimum repayment, your extra contribution and the minimum repayment from the first-place debt in your stack, which is now paid off.

5. Continue this pattern until all debts are paid off.

Once all your debts are paid off, you will have a consistent amount available per month that you can contribute towards your savings goals.

> **EXPLORE YOUR OPTIONS**
>
> ## Investigate your borrowing power
>
> Use the tables below to investigate what happens to your borrowing power once you've paid off your debts or as your income increases. You can use any bank's online home loan borrowing calculator to work out your maximum borrowing power. (I find the Commonwealth Bank Borrowing Tool particularly user friendly. Google 'CBA Borrowing Power Calculator'.)
>
> | Annual pre-tax income | Total monthly repayments of personal loans and student loans (HELP) | Total credit card limits | Your max. borrowing power at a 6% p.a. interest rate |
> |---|---|---|---|
> |  |  |  |  |
>
> *(continued)*

How would your borrowing power change if you had paid off your personal loans and cancelled your credit cards? We will assume that you still have a student debt.

| Annual pre-tax income | Total monthly repayments of personal loans and student loans (HELP) | Total credit card limits | Your max. borrowing power at a 6% p.a. interest rate |
|---|---|---|---|
|  |  |  |  |

Now calculate what you could borrow if you still had all your current debt and credit card limits, but you were earning $20 000 more before tax per year.

| Annual pre-tax income + $20 000 | Total monthly repayments of personal loans and students loans (HELP) | Total credit card limits | Your max. borrowing power at a 6% p.a. interest rate |
|---|---|---|---|
|  |  |  |  |

Finally, investigate what you could borrow if you had paid off your personal loans and cancelled your credit cards *and* your current income was increased by $20 000.

| Annual pre-tax income + $20 000 | Total monthly repayments of personal loans and students loans (HELP) | Total credit card limits | Your max. borrowing power at a 6% p.a. interest rate |
|---|---|---|---|
|  |  |  |  |

For a reminder on ways to increase your income, flick back to chapter 3.

This chapter gave you an insight into how a bank calculates your maximum borrowing power. Understanding how your living expenses and liabilities impact your ability to buy a home should empower you to make changes to your financial situation before you apply for a home loan. If you are starting to take control of your income, then in conjunction with debt stacking, you should be able to borrow enough money to buy your first home in the near future. But remember, if you don't start today, you may well find the housing market in your city becomes out of reach.

## CASE STUDY

## Lin's home-buying journey

Lin completed his apprenticeship as a welder in 2023. Throughout his apprenticeship he committed to a savings plan, reaching his goal of saving $60 000.

With his apprenticeship behind him, Lin would be earning a lot more, and he wanted to treat himself. After looking at several second-hand utes, Lin test-drove a brand new Toyota Land Cruiser and quickly decided that was the car for him. He negotiated a price of $140 000 drive away including all the bells and whistles. Lin contributed $40 000 from his savings and secured a $100 000 car loan to pay the balance. Now, at the age of 25 and with $33 000 in savings, Lin wants to buy his first home.

### Lin's financial snapshot

| Annual before-tax income | $132 000 | Monthly living expenses | $2500 |
|---|---|---|---|
| Job title | Welder | Total credit card limits | $8000 |

*(continued)*

| Total savings | $33 000 | Monthly personal loan repayments | $1781 |
|---|---|---|---|
| Eligible for government support | Yes | Monthly student debt repayments | $0 |
| Parent guarantor | Yes | Residency status | Australian citizen |

## Lin's outcome

Lin assumed he was in a strong financial position considering he was earning more than any of his mates. Based on his income, and assuming he had no liabilities, Lin could borrow $624 000 for a home loan. This would be enough to achieve his goal of buying a one-bedroom apartment in Sydney.

However, Lin's car loan repayments, coupled with his credit card debt and monthly personal loan repayments has decreased his maximum borrowing power by $206 000, down to only $418 000. Despite his savings of $33 000, his eligibility for all the first home buyer incentives and the fact his parents are willing to be guarantors, Lin's borrowing power isn't enough to buy a property in Sydney. Lin is yet to purchase a home and is now considering selling his Land Cruiser for substantially less than he paid for it.

# Key takeaways
# for your home-buying journey

- Banks calculate your after-tax income minus your monthly liabilities and living expenses to determine how much you could afford towards home loan repayments. This figure is then used to establish your maximum borrowing power (pending interest rates).

- The higher your living expenses and repayments towards liabilities, the lower your maximum home loan borrowing power.

- Personal loans can be classified as secured or unsecured. A secured personal loan is a loan guaranteed by an asset such as a car. An unsecured personal loan is where no asset is provided as security.

- Credit card limits are used by the bank when calculating your maximum home loan borrowing power. This is because you could max out your credit card after securing a home loan, forcing you to repay the maximum monthly amount and potentially affecting your ability to meet your home loan repayments.

- While they won't directly affect your borrowing power, Buy Now Pay Later debts can impact your home loan application by revealing your spending habits.

- Students loans such as HELP debts will reduce your maximum home loan borrowing power. Your annual pre-tax income defines your HELP debt repayment, which is used to calculate the reduction in your home loan borrowing power.

- The debt-stacking strategy can be used to order your debts from highest to lowest interest and pay them off as quickly as possible. Reducing your liabilities will increase your maximum home loan borrowing power.

# 6 | HOW MUCH do you need in SAVINGS?

My first ever meeting with a home loan consultant at one of the major banks left me completely deflated. They told me that I would need at least $40 000 to buy a $400 000 house. With only half that amount in savings, I left with my tail between my legs. A few weeks later I was sharing this story with a friend who said that his older sister had just bought a $400 000 home with only $25 000 in the bank. Either my mate was full of it, or the bank hadn't given me all my options.

Determined to get answers, I approached a different bank. This bank said I was up for $30 000 in deposit and upfront fees to buy my first home. The next bank said $35 000 and the last bank I had a meeting with said $25 000. Through this process, I came to realise that banks' lending requirements differ, and as a result the required deposit size varies from bank to bank. Some banks allow you to borrow up to 90 per cent of the home value. Others will let you borrow up to 98 per cent of the home value. These percentages are known as the 'loan to value ratio', or LVR.

The LVR a bank requires for its home loan products heavily impacts how much you need to save.

In this chapter I'm going to teach you how to take advantage of first home-buyer incentives to minimise the amount of savings you need so you can enter the housing market as soon as possible.

## Your home loan deposit

The savings you need to accumulate to purchase your first home can be separated into two parts: the deposit and the upfront costs. (We'll look at the upfront costs—in particular stamp duty, the biggest component—later in the chapter.)

The home loan deposit is your initial contribution to the purchase price of a property. For example, if you were to buy a $600 000 home with a deposit of $30 000, then you would have a home loan of $570 000. This represents an LVR of 95 per cent. In the eyes of the bank, as your deposit percentage increases, your risk profile decreases.

## Lenders mortgage insurance (LMI)

When a bank offers you a home loan, it is taking a calculated risk. The bank determines the amount of risk by asking two questions:

1. What's the likelihood that you'll be able to make your monthly repayments for the life of the loan?

2. If you were unable to meet your repayments and the bank was forced to take possession of the property, would it make a loss after selling it?

As we saw in chapter 5, banks will analyse your spending habits and current liabilities vs your income to determine whether you'll be able to make your monthly loan repayments.

In addition, to be classified as a low-risk applicant, you would need a deposit worth at least 20 per cent of the property's value. A deposit of this size gives the bank a large enough buffer to mitigate the risk of a loss, even if property prices were to drop.

For a bank to justify offering you a home loan with less than a 20 per cent deposit, it needs to take out an insurance policy from a third party. This is called lenders mortgage insurance (LMI) and it protects the bank from incurring a loss if you default on your loan and it has to sell your property. But beware: this is not an insurance policy that protects you, the homebuyer, in any way. What's more, you will be expected to pay the one-off premium, either upfront or by adding it to your home loan.

The higher your LVR, the higher your LMI premium. In other words, the smaller your deposit is, the higher your LMI fee will be. Table 6.1 (overleaf) outlines approximately what your LMI fee would be on a $600 000 property purchase. It's important to note that this figure can vary slightly depending on the bank as well as the state/territory you're in.

**Table 6.1: approximate LMI premiums on a property valued at $600 000, based on various deposit sizes**

| Deposit size | Deposit as a percentage of a $600 000 purchase | Approx. LMI premium |
|---|---|---|
| $120 000 | 20% | $0 |
| $105 000 | 17.5% | $4000 |
| $90 000 | 15% | $8000 |
| $75 000 | 12.5% | $11 000 |
| $60 000 | 10% | $15 000 |
| $45 000 | 7.5% | $25 000 |
| $30 000 | 5% | $27 500 |

Yes, LMI can be expensive! Not only is the premium higher as if your deposit is smaller, but it also increases as properties become more expensive. Someone buying an $800 000 property at 95 per cent LVR will pay more for LMI than someone buying a $700 000 property at 95 per cent LVR. The good news is, there are ways to avoid paying LMI, even if you've only saved a 5 per cent deposit.

One way of avoiding LMI, is by having a third party guarantee that they will pay the bank 20 per cent of the property value if the bank has to sell the property and incurs a loss. Most first home buyers utilising a guarantor ask their parents to take on this role. Those who don't have that option can apply for the government to become their guarantor by securing a spot in a first home buyer program (you'll read about these programs next).

If none of the above are possible, is it worth biting the bullet and paying LMI to enter the housing market? In short, absolutely!

As of July 2024, average rent across the eight capital cities in Australia is $630 per week. That's $32 760 per year that a tenant is paying off someone else's mortgage. If you were able to save $200 a week on top of paying your rent, it would take you 600 weeks, or just over 11 and a half years, to save a 20 per cent deposit for a $600 000 home. What do you think is going to happen to house prices over that 11-year time frame? What type of home will you be able to buy for $600 000 in 11 years? Get into the market while you can, despite LMI, to reap the rewards of capital growth over time.

## Government home-buyer programs

The Australian Government recognises how challenging it is to buy your first home. It also understands how hard it is to re-enter the housing market after a relationship breakdown. In response to this, it has created several programs that can assist you in purchasing a home. Utilising one or more of these programs could save you tens of thousands of dollars, so dog-ear the next few pages: your bank account will love you for it.

### *First Home Buyer Guarantee (FHBG)*

Under the First Home Buyer Guarantee (FHBG), part of an eligible home-buyer's home loan is guaranteed by Housing Australia. This enables you to buy a home with as little as a 5 per cent deposit, without needing to pay LMI. Since the government guarantees up to 15 per cent of your home loan, the participating bank will deem your home loan low risk and treat it like someone buying a home with a 20 per cent deposit. When the government becomes your guarantor, it does not take any ownership of your home. This means, if you sell the property in the future, you do not owe it any portion of the profits. As a guarantor, it doesn't contribute to the purchase of the property or any portion of the repayments. However, your home loan amount will be 95 per cent of the purchase property's value if you contribute the minimum 5 per cent deposit.

On 1 July 2024, 35 000 FHBG places were released Australia-wide. Any remaining places will expire on 30 June 2025. The program is designed to help the home buyers who need it the most, so you must meet the following eligibility criteria to take advantage of the FHBG:

- If buying as a single applicant, your annual income before tax must be under $125 000.

- If buying as joint applicants, your annual income before tax must be under $200 000.

- All applicants must be either Australian citizens, permanent residents or New Zealand citizens living in Australia.

- No applicant may have owned a home for at least 10 years prior to making a purchase using the FHBG.

- You must intend to be the owner-occupier of the purchased property.

The FHBG operates in all states and territories across Australia. However, maximum purchase prices (i.e. property price caps) apply. These caps vary depending on location—see table 6.2.

You can use the FHBG to buy an existing house, townhouse, unit or apartment; secure a house-and-land package; purchase land with a separate contract to build; and for off-the-plan apartments and townhouses.

Table 6.2: First Home Buyer Guarantee (FHBG) property price caps

| State | Capital city and regional centres* | Rest of state |
|---|---|---|
| NSW | $900 000 | $750 000 |
| Vic. | $800 000 | $650 000 |
| QLD | $700 000 | $550 000 |
| WA | $600 000 | $450 000 |
| SA | $600 000 | $450 000 |
| Tas. | $600 000 | $450 000 |
| ACT | $750 000 | $750 000 |
| NT | $600 000 | $600 000 |
| Jervis Bay Territory and Norfolk Island | $550 000 | $550 000 |
| Christmas Island and Cocos (Keeling) Islands | $400 000 | $400 000 |

*Regional centres are Newcastle, Lake Macquarie, the Illawarra, Geelong, the Gold Coast and the Sunshine Coast.

To check what your maximum price cap is, based on your desired postcode, you can use the online calculator on the Housing Australia website. Search for 'property price caps'.

The biggest benefit of the FHBG is that you will not be charged LMI. As you saw in table 6.1, this can save you upfront costs of up to $27 500 on a property worth $600 000. If you were to add this on to your home loan—including the interest that will accumulate on this fee—you could save even more.

With limited spots available in this program, it's important to reach out to a mortgage broker who can find you a bank that has places available. It's also important to note that as of writing, in July of 2024, no commitment has been made by the government regarding the renewal of the FHBG into the 2025–26 financial year, so take advantage of this program while you can.

## *Regional First Home Buyer Guarantee (RFHBG)*

The Regional First Home Buyer Guarantee (RFHBG) is a replica of the FHBG. The eligibility criteria are the same. However, the RFHBG is designed specifically for first home buyers wanting to purchase a property in a regional area. On 1 July 2024, 10 000 spots were released for the 2024–25 financial year. The RFHBG operates in all states and territories across Australia, and maximum purchase prices (property price caps) also apply here. Table 6.3 sets out the price caps, which vary based on location.

**Table 6.3: Regional First Home Buyer Guarantee (RFHBG) property price caps**

| State | Regional centre* | All other regional areas |
| --- | --- | --- |
| NSW | $900 000 | $750 000 |
| Vic. | $800 000 | $650 000 |
| QLD | $700 000 | $550 000 |
| WA | | $450 000 |
| SA | | $450 000 |
| Tas. | | $450 000 |
| ACT | | $750 000 |

| State | Regional centre* | All other regional areas |
|---|---|---|
| NT | | $600 000 |
| Jervis Bay Territory and Norfolk Island | | $550 000 |
| Christmas Island and Cocos (Keeling) Islands | | $400 000 |

*Regional centres are Newcastle, Lake Macquarie, the Illawarra, Geelong, the Gold Coast and the Sunshine Coast.

To check if a desired postcode is eligible for the RFHBG, go to the Housing Australia website and search for 'property price caps'.

## *Family Home Guarantee (FHG)*

The Family Home Guarantee (FHG) aims to support single parents or single legal guardians with at least one dependant to buy a home. This program operates in a similar fashion to the FHBG in that the government guarantees a portion of your home loan, negating the need for your bank to charge you LMI.

The key difference is that you only need a 2 per cent deposit because the government will guarantee up to 18 per cent of the purchase property's value. In addition, you are allowed to have previously owned a property in Australia. The government recognises that it's likely a couple who have separated may have owned a home within the last 10 years, so they have removed this eligibility restriction, enabling single parents to more easily re-enter the housing market. On 1 July 2024, 5000 spots were released for the 2024–25 financial year. You must meet the following eligibility criteria to take advantage of the FHG:

- You must apply as an individual.

- Your annual income before tax must be under $125 000.

- You must be an Australian citizen, a permanent resident or a New Zealand citizen living in Australia.

- You must be a single parent or single legal guardian of at least one dependant. A person is considered single if they do not have a spouse and/or de facto partner. It's important to note, if you are separated but not divorced, you are not classified as single under the eligibility criteria for the FHG.

- You intend to be the owner-occupier of the purchased property.

- You must not currently own property or, upon settlement of the guaranteed property, not be intending to own a separate property.

You can access a short questionnaire via the Housing Australia website to determine whether you're eligible for the FHG. Search for 'eligibility tool'.

The FHG operates in all states and territories across Australia. However, as for the FHBG and RFHBG, maximum property price caps apply, and they vary depending on location. These property price caps are the same as those for the FHBG (see table 6.4). You can use the FHG to buy an existing house, townhouse, unit or apartment; secure a house-and-land package; purchase land with a separate contract to build; and for off-the-plan apartments or townhouses.

Table 6.4: Family Home Guarantee (FHG) property price caps

| State | Capital city and regional centres* | Rest of state |
| --- | --- | --- |
| NSW | $900 000 | $750 000 |
| Vic. | $800 000 | $650 000 |
| QLD | $700 000 | $550 000 |
| WA | $600 000 | $450 000 |
| SA | $600 000 | $450 000 |
| Tas. | $600 000 | $450 000 |
| ACT | $750 000 | $750 000 |
| NT | $600 000 | $600 000 |
| Jervis Bay Territory and Norfolk Island | $550 000 | $550 000 |
| Christmas Island and Cocos (Keeling) Islands | $400 000 | $400 000 |

*Regional centres are Newcastle, Lake Macquarie, the Illawarra, Geelong, the Gold Coast and the Sunshine Coast.

In addition to not having to pay LMI, single parents wanting to buy a home under the FHG only need to save a 2 per cent deposit. However, this means they must be able to service a home loan of 98 per cent of the purchased property's value. So, a $500 000 home would result in a $490 000 home loan.

## *Shared equity schemes*

In response to first home buyers being limited by their maximum home loan borrowing power, Australian state and territory governments have created shared equity schemes. Unlike the home guarantee programs, where the government becomes your guarantor, under a shared equity scheme, the government will purchase a portion of your property. With the government purchasing up to 25 per cent of your property, you only need to contribute a 5 per cent deposit. You will not be charged LMI, and you will be left with a loan of 70 per cent of the property's value. Your monthly loan repayments will reflect this lower mortgage amount.

The negative is that the government owns a portion of your home. This means, if you want to sell it in the future, you will need to pay the government its share of the profits. As your property either increases or decreases in value over time, so does its share of your property. The Federal Government has proposed a nation-wide shared equity scheme, which, as of July 2024, is awaiting approval in the senate. The New South Wales Government had created a shared equity scheme, but retired it on 30 June 2024. However, the Victorian Government has implemented and recently expanded its own shared equity scheme, called the Victorian Homebuyer Fund. Read on to find out how it works.

## Victorian Homebuyer Fund

If you have a 5 per cent deposit, the Victorian Government will contribute up to 25 per cent of the purchase price in exchange for an equity share in the property. In line with the proposed federal shared equity scheme, the Victorian Homebuyer Fund saves you money by reducing your mortgage amount and removing the need for LMI. Aboriginal and Torres Strait Islander peoples only need a 3.5 per cent deposit and qualify for up to a 35 per cent shared equity payment.

You will be expected to buy back the government's share in your property over time, either by refinancing, using your savings or when you sell the property. You won't be charged interest, but the Victorian Government will be entitled to share in any capital gains or losses proportionate to its share in the property.

To be eligible for the Victorian Homebuyer Fund:

- you must be over 18

- you must be an individual first home buyer, not a company or trust

- all applicants must be permanent residents, Australian citizens or New Zealanders holding a special category visa. New Zealand citizens must be living in Australia at the time when the eligible transaction is completed

- you must have a single income before tax of under $135 155

- you must have a combined income before tax of under $216 245 for joint applicants as well as for single parents

- no applicant may hold any interest in any land in Australia or overseas

- no applicant may hold shares in a private company that holds any interest in any land in Australia or overseas

- all applicants must live in the property as their primary place of residence (PPR)

- you must not be buying the property from a person or entity who is related to you

- participants may purchase an eligible property anywhere in Victoria. However, it must be a standard residential property such as a house, townhouse, unit or apartment—not vacant land. The maximum purchase price allowed in metropolitan Melbourne and Geelong is $950 000. In regional Victoria the maximum allowed is $700 000

- you may purchase an existing property or a new one, as long as a certificate of occupancy is issued prior to the date on the contract of sale. As such, off-the-plan property purchases are not eligible. The property must be vacant when purchased. If it is rented out, the lease must end within 12 months of the date of purchase and any tenants must vacate the property.

In my opinion, the biggest negative of the Victoria Homebuyer Fund is your ongoing obligations. Every year, you must prove you are still eligible for the funding by completing a review and providing supporting information. Supporting documents include a certificate of currency of insurance, payslips, tax returns, home loan statements and utility bills. Also, you are obliged to notify the government within 10 business days if your circumstances change at any time.

Your property must be insured at all times, and you must pay bills such as council rates, utilities, body corporate fees, stamp duty and home loan repayments on time. You may not make any modifications or do any renovations that cost more than $10 000 without approval. Likewise, nothing that involves structural changes or requires authorisation (e.g. council approval) can be made without approval. In addition, if you wish to refinance or sell your property—or make voluntary payments that result in you exiting the Victorian Homebuyer Fund within the first 2 years—you must gain approval from the government.

You must start repaying the Victorian Homebuyer Fund's interest in your property if any of the following occurs:

- Your pre-tax annual income exceeds the threshold on two consecutive annual review reporting dates.

- You receive an inheritance or lotto win (or a similar windfall) of $10 000 or more.

- You have made a mandatory payment and your before-tax annual income at the next reporting date has increased by 10 per cent; and your bank has approved an increase of your home loan. The loan increase will only be approved if it enables you to make a payment that reduces the government's share by at least 5 per cent—for example, from 25 per cent to 20 per cent—and it is at least $10 000.

You may make voluntary extra repayments to start repaying the government's share provided each repayment reduces the government's share by at least 5 per cent. If you sell your property, the money will be distributed to the following entities in this order:

1. *your bank*—to pay off your remaining home loan

2. *the government*—to pay back its share in your property

3. *anyone else with a legal or equitable interest in the property*—for example, the council if rate payments are not up to date

4. *you.*

I reckon you've probably realised something: the Victoria Home Buyer Fund comes with a shitload of conditions! In my opinion, it's only designed for those people who are completely priced out of the market and could never enter without the government buying 25 per cent of their property. If you have the borrowing power, utilising one of the home guarantee programs will allow you to buy with the same-size deposit of 5 per cent and you will not be restricted by these overwhelming conditions.

## *First Home Owner Grant (FHOG)*

The FHOG is a national scheme funded by the states and territories of Australia and administered under their own legislations. Under the scheme, a one-off grant is payable to first home buyers who satisfy the eligibility criteria. In all states and territories only one grant is payable per eligible transaction, so two people purchasing a house together may only receive one grant. However, the amount payable and the eligibility criteria vary from state to state.

## New South Wales

In New South Wales you may be eligible for an FHOG of $10 000 if you are buying a newly built or substantially renovated home. The purchase price must not be more than $600 000.

If you buy vacant land and sign a building contract, you may be eligible for an FHOG based on the combined value of the vacant land *plus* the value of the comprehensive home building contract *plus* the cost of any building variations that are not valued at more than $750 000.

If you buy a home that was substantially renovated by the existing owner and the purchase price is not more than $600 000, you may be eligible for the grant if:

- most of the home was replaced or removed

- the seller, a builder or a tenant did not live in the home prior to, during or after the renovations

- it is the first time the home has been sold since completion of the renovations.

If the person who built the home lived in it, leased it out or used it for short-term accommodation, it is not considered a new home the first time it is for sale.

The FHOG can be combined with other home-buyer programs, such as the FHBG.

To be eligible for the FHOG in New South Wales:

- each applicant must be over 18

- you must be an individual first home buyer, not a company or trust

- at least one applicant must be a permanent resident, Australian citizen or New Zealander holding a special category visa. New Zealand citizens must be living in Australia at the time when the eligible transaction is completed

- you, your spouse, partner or co-purchaser may not have owned a home before 1 July 2000

- you must occupy your first home as your principal place of residence (PPR) within 12 months of construction or purchase, and for a minimum of 12 continuous months.

You will not be eligible for the FHOG if:

- you have already received an FHOG in Australia

- you owned a home or other residential property in Australia — either jointly or separately — before 1 July 2000

- you lived in a home in Australia that you owned, wholly or partially, for 6 continuous months or more, on or after 1 July 2000. However, you or your spouse may be eligible for the FHOG if you purchased a residential property after 1 July 2000 and didn't live in it for more than 6 continuous months.

To learn more about the FHOG in New South Wales, or to apply for the grant, head to the Revenue NSW website and search for 'FHOG'.

## Victoria

In Victoria you can claim a $10 000 First Home Owner Grant (FHOG) when you buy or build your first new home. This policy is similar to that in New South Wales in that your first new home can be a house, townhouse, unit or apartment. It may be a substantially renovated home or one built to replace a demolished premises. It may not be an investment property or a holiday home. The contract price must be $750 000 or less.

If you are buying off-the-plan, the contract price—not the dutiable value—must be $750 000 or less. If you are building a home, the contract-to-build price must be $750 000 or less. If the person who built the home lived in it, leased it out or used it for short-term accommodation, it is not considered a new home the first time it is for sale.

The FHOG can be combined with other home-buyer programs, such as the FHBG.

To be eligible for the FHOG in Victoria:

- at least one applicant must be over 18
- you must be an individual first home buyer, not a company or trust

- at least one applicant must be a permanent resident, Australian citizen or New Zealander holding a special category visa. New Zealand citizens must be living in Australia at the time when the eligible transaction is completed

- you, your spouse, partner or co-purchaser may not have owned a home before 1 July 2000

- you must occupy your first home as your PPR within 12 months of construction or purchase and for a minimum of 12 continuous months.

You will not be eligible for the FHOG if:

- you have already received an FHOG in Australia

- you owned a home or other residential property in Australia — either jointly or separately — before 1 July 2000

- you lived in a home in Australia that you owned, wholly or partially, for 6 continuous months or more, on or after 1 July 2000. However, you or your spouse may be eligible for the FHOG if you purchased a residential property after 1 July 2000 and didn't live in it for more than 6 continuous months.

To learn more about the FHOG in Victoria, or to apply for the grant, head to the Victorian State Revenue Office website and search for 'FHOG'.

## Queensland

Queensland offers a much more generous First Home Owner Grant (FHOG) than New South Wales and Victoria. For buying or building a new home, the grant amount is $30 000 for a contract signed between 20 November 2023 and 30 June 2025 or $15 000 for a contract signed before 20 November 2023. You must be buying or building a new home valued at less than $750 000, including land and any contract variations.

For a transaction to be eligible, the following applies:

- The home must not have been sold as a place of residence or lived in prior to the time of completion.

- The home is classified as a house, unit, duplex or townhouse; or a detached dwelling such as a granny flat or tiny home built on a relative's land.

- The home has been moved from one site to another (this includes kit homes and modular homes).

- The home is in a manufactured home park.

- The home is substantially renovated.

- The home must be either a new home or an off-the-plan purchase. It can also be a substantial renovation, contract-to-build or owner-builder home.

The FHOG can be combined with other home-buyer programs, such as the FHBG.

To be eligible for the FHOG in Queensland:

- each applicant must be over 18

- at least one applicant must be a permanent resident, Australian citizen or New Zealander holding a special category visa. New Zealand citizens must be living in Australia at the time when the eligible transaction is completed

- you must occupy your first home as your principal place of residence (PPR) within 12 months of construction or purchase and for a minimum of 6 continuous months.

You will not be eligible for the FHOG if:

- you have already received an FHOG in Australia

- you owned a home or other residential property in Australia — either jointly or separately — before 1 July 2000

- you lived in a home in Australia that you owned, wholly or partially, on or after 1 July 2000.

To learn more about the FHOG in Queensland, or to apply for the grant, head to the Queensland Revenue Office website and search for 'FHOG'.

## Western Australia

In Western Australia you can claim a $10 000 First Home Owner Grant (FHOG) when you buy or build your first new home. This policy is similar to Victoria in that your first new home can be a house, townhouse, unit or apartment. It may be a substantially renovated home or one built to replace a demolished premises. It may not be an investment property or a holiday home.

To be eligible, the total transaction value may not exceed the capped amount. The cap varies depending on the location of the home. For a contract-to-build, a new home or an off-the-plan purchase it needs to be located:

- south of the 26th parallel of south latitude (this covers all Perth metropolitan areas) and the combined value of land and building may not exceed $750 000

- north of the 26th parallel of south latitude and the combined value of land and building may not exceed $1 000 000.

The FHOG can be combined with other home-buyer programs, such as the FHBG.

To be eligible for the FHOG in Western Australia:

- at least one applicant must be over 18

- you must be an individual first home buyer, not a company or trust

- at least one applicant must be a permanent resident, Australian citizen or New Zealander holding a special category visa. New Zealand citizens must be living in Australia at the time when the eligible transaction is completed

- you, your spouse, partner or co-purchaser may not have owned a home before 1 July 2000

- you must occupy your first home as your principal place of residence (PPR) within 12 months of construction or purchase and for a minimum of 6 continuous months.

You will not be eligible for the FHOG if:

- you have already received an FHOG in Australia

- you owned a home or other residential property in Australia—either jointly or separately—before 1 July 2000

- you owned a residential property in Australia on or after 1 July 2000 and you occupied that property as a PPR before 1 July 2004

- you owned residential property in Australia on or after 1 July 2000 and you occupied that property as a PPR for a continuous period of at least 6 months beginning on or after 1 July 2004. However, you or your spouse may still be eligible for the FHOG if you purchased a residential property after 1 July 2000 and did not live there as your PPR.

To learn more about the FHOG in Western Australia, or to apply for the grant, head to the Government of Western Australia website and search for 'FHOG'.

## South Australia

In South Australia a grant of $15 000 is payable to first home buyers eligible for the First Home Owner Grant (FHOG). Just like the other states, you must be buying or building a new home—a house, flat, unit, townhouse or apartment—and it must become your primary place of residence (PPR). On 6 June 2024, the South Australian Government removed the property value cap for the FHOG. However, if you signed a contract to buy or build a new home between 15 June 2023 and 5 June 2024, a market value cap of $650 000 will apply.

The FHOG can be combined with other home-buyer programs, such as the FHBG.

To be eligible for the FHOG in South Australia:

- at least one applicant must be over 18
- you must be an individual first home buyer, not a company or trust
- at least one applicant must be a permanent resident, Australian citizen or New Zealander holding a special category visa. New Zealand citizens must be living in Australia at the time when the eligible transaction is completed
- you, your spouse, partner or co-purchaser may not have owned a home before 1 July 2000
- you must occupy your first home as your PPR within 12 months of construction or purchase and for a minimum of 6 continuous months.

You will not be eligible for the FHOG if:

- you have already received an FHOG in Australia

- you owned a home or other residential property in Australia — either jointly or separately — before 1 July 2000

- you lived in a home in Australia that you owned, wholly or partially, for 6 continuous months or more, on or after 1 July 2000. However, you or your spouse may be eligible for the FHOG if you purchased a residential property after 1 July 2000 and didn't live in it as your PPR.

To learn more about the FHOG in South Australia, or to apply for the grant, head to the Revenue SA website and search for 'FHOG'.

## Tasmania

In Tasmania, as of 1 July 2024, you could be eligible for a $10 000 payment under the First Home Owner Grant (FHOG). Transactions that commenced between 1 April 2021 and 30 June 2024 were eligible for $30 000. There are no property value caps applicable to gain access to the grant as long as you are buying or building a new house, townhouse, unit or apartment.

To be eligible:

- at least one applicant must be over 18

- you must be an individual first home buyer, not a company or trust

- at least one applicant must be a permanent resident, Australian citizen or New Zealander holding a special category visa. New Zealand citizens must be living in Australia at the time when the eligible transaction is completed

- you, your spouse, partner or co-purchaser may not have owned a home before 1 July 2000

- you must occupy your first home as your principal place of residence (PPR) within 12 months of construction or purchase and for a minimum of 6 continuous months.

You will not be eligible for the FHOG if:

- you have already received an FHOG in Australia

- you owned a home or other residential property in Australia—either jointly or separately—before 1 July 2000

- you lived in a home in Australia that you owned, wholly or partially, for 6 continuous months or more on or after 1 July 2000. However, you or your spouse may be eligible for the FHOG if you purchased a residential property after 1 July 2000 and didn't live in it as your home.

To learn more about the First Home Owner Grant in Tasmania, or to apply for the grant, head to the State Revenue Office of Tasmania website and search for FHOG.

## Australian Capital Territory

As of 30 June 2019, the ACT Government scrapped the First Home Owner Grant (FHOG) and replaced it with the Home Buyer Concession Scheme. This scheme relates to a concession paid on stamp duty when buying a property as a first home buyer. Stamp duty will be unpacked further in the 'Upfront costs' section of this chapter.

## Northern Territory

In the Northern Territory you could be eligible for a $10 000 First Home Owner Grant (FHOG) if you choose to buy or build a new home. Your income and the price of the home do not affect the FHOG. A new home is one that has never been lived in or sold as a place of residence.

The FHOG can be combined with other home-buyer programs, such as the FHBG.

To be eligible for the FHOG in the Northern Territory:

- you must be over 18

- at least one applicant must be a permanent resident, Australian citizen or New Zealander holding a special category visa. New Zealand citizens must be living in Australia at the time when the eligible transaction is completed

- you must occupy your first home as your principal place of residence (PPR) within 12 months of construction or purchase and for a minimum of 6 continuous months.

You will not be eligible for the FHOG if:

- you have previously received an FHOG in Australia

- you owned a home or other residential property in Australia — either jointly or separately — before 1 July 2000

- you lived in a home in Australia that you owned, wholly or partially, on or after 1 July 2000.

To learn more about the FHOG in the Northern Territory, or to apply for the grant, head to the Northern Territory Government Information and Services website and search for 'FHOG'.

## *Guarantor home loans*

As I mentioned earlier in this chapter, there is a way you can buy a home with absolutely no savings in the bank. Using this strategy, you will not have to contribute any savings towards a deposit or the upfront costs. This pathway to home ownership is by far the shortest because you don't need to spend years building up your savings account.

A guarantor home loan involves a family member offering equity in their own home as additional security for your loan. The usable equity in a family member's home is calculated by subtracting their outstanding mortgage from 80 per cent of the value of their home. If you secure a home loan guaranteed by a family member's property, it also means you will not be charged LMI. To understand how it works let's look at an example.

## CASE STUDY

## Sethuki's parents become her guarantors

Sethuki wants to buy a home costing $600 000. As a first home buyer in Victoria, she can claim a full stamp duty exemption on a $600 000 purchase, reducing her stamp duty to $0 — I'll explain how this works shortly. Additional upfront costs, including conveyancing, total $3000. To avoid LMI, Sethuki would need to pay a 20 per cent deposit, equalling $120 000. The deposit, combined with the upfront costs, totals $123 000. She does not have any savings to contribute to the deposit or the upfront costs, so she has asked her parents to become her guarantors.

Sethuki's parents have agreed to become her guarantors. They own a home worth $800 000. To become guarantors, they must retain at least 20 per cent equity in their home after the security for Sethuki's purchase has been calculated. Sethuki's parents currently have an outstanding mortgage of $500 000 on their home loan. To determine whether they have enough equity to become Sethuki's guarantors, the bank adds the deposit and upfront costs total of $123 000 to her parents' mortgage, giving a total of $623 000. The bank will approve this security if the combined total is less than 80 per cent of her parents' home value. Since $623 000 is 77.88 per cent of $800 000, Sethuki will be able to use her parents' equity as security to purchase the $600 000 property, pending approval of her home loan.

In this scenario, Sethuki will be making repayments for the total loan amount, including the portion secured against her parents' property. As such, she will need to be approved for a $603 000 home loan against a purchase value of $600 000. Her parents would not need to refinance their home loan, nor would their monthly repayments increase. Their outstanding mortgage amount will not increase.

> They have simply agreed that if Sethuki were unable to make repayments on her mortgage—resulting in the bank repossessing the property—they would cover any loss incurred by the bank up to 20 per cent of the value of Sethuki's total mortgage.

The role of a guarantor is generally limited to immediate family members of the home buyer. Usually, this is a parent, but guarantors can also include siblings and grandparents. Some banks will allow extended family members to be guarantors, but this varies depending on the lender.

Guarantors take on a level of risk. But there is a common misconception that they are locked in to the role of guarantor for the full 30-year term of the loan. The fact is that once the purchased property increases by 20 per cent in value, the purchaser can apply to refinance the home loan. It's through this refinancing process that guarantors and their equity can be released from their role as guarantor. How long it takes for the property to gain 20 per cent in value will determine how long a guarantor will be attached to the mortgage.

As a parent of two young children, I worry about the property market they'll be forced to navigate in 25 years from now. I anticipate that house prices will continue to outpace wage growth. That's why I'm preparing myself now by working hard to pay off my mortgage so that I can help my children buy their first home by becoming their guarantor. My role as a parent will not stop when my kids turn 18. I will continue to be the safety net that enables them to take risks, experiment with different careers and build a home for their own families one day.

# Upfront costs

The largest component of your upfront costs when purchasing a home is property tax, also known as stamp duty. Other upfront costs include land office administration fees, conveyancing and agents' fees.

## *Stamp duty*

Stamp duty is the property tax that you pay to the government. The amount of stamp duty you pay varies depending on the value of the property you're buying. The more expensive the purchase, the more you pay in stamp duty. To reduce the amount of savings required to enter the housing market, several state governments and territories have implemented a stamp duty exemption scheme for first home buyers, heavily discounting—and in some cases completely erasing—stamp duty costs. This scheme can be used in conjunction with the First Home Guarantee and/or the First Home Owners Grant and/or parent guarantors.

### New South Wales

In New South Wales you are entitled to a full stamp duty exemption if you are purchasing a new or existing home valued up to $800 000. Homes valued between $800 000 and $1 000 000 may qualify for a concessional rate. If you are buying vacant land and plan to build a home on it, you may be entitled to a land exemption valued up to $350 000. For land valued between $350 000 and $450 000 you may be entitled to a concessional rate.

To be eligible for the stamp duty exemption or concession in New South Wales:

- the purchase can be for a new or existing home, or vacant land, in New South Wales
- the value of the property must be within the threshold amounts
- you must be over 18
- you must be an individual, not a company or trust
- you and your spouse/partner may not have ever owned or co-owned residential property in Australia
- you and your spouse/partner may not have previously received an exemption or concession under the scheme
- at least one of the first home buyers must be an Australian citizen or permanent resident
- you must occupy the home as your PPR within 12 months of construction or purchase and for a minimum of 12 continuous months.

To learn more about the stamp duty exemption policy in New South Wales, head to the Revenue NSW website and search for 'first home buyers assistance scheme'.

Table 6.5 (overleaf) outlines the amount of stamp duty and additional upfront costs payable as a first home buyer utilising either an exemption or concession.

Table 6.5: first home buyer exemption/concession amounts on stamp duty in New South Wales

| NSW home value | Stamp duty | Approx. additional upfront costs | Approx. total upfront costs |
|---|---|---|---|
| $500 000 | $0 | $1000 | $1000 |
| $600 000 | $0 | $1200 | $1200 |
| $700 000 | $0 | $1400 | $1400 |
| $800 000 | $0 | $1600 | $1600 |
| $900 000 | $19 868 | $1800 | $21 668 |
| $1 000 000 | $39 735 | $2000 | $41 735 |

## Victoria

As a first home buyer in Victoria you can claim a full stamp duty exemption for properties valued $600 000 or less and a stamp duty concession for properties valued between $600 001 and $750 000. The stamp duty concession works on a sliding scale. The closer the value of the home is to $600 001, the greater the concession. The home can be new or established (unlike for the FHOG). The exemption also applies to vacant land.

To be eligible for the stamp duty exemption or concession in Victoria:

- at least one applicant must be over 18

- you must be a first home buyer, buying as an individual, not a company or trust

- at least one applicant must be a permanent resident, Australian citizen or New Zealander holding a special category visa. New Zealand citizens must be living in Australia at the time when the eligible transaction is completed

- you, your spouse, partner or co-purchaser may not have owned a home before 1 July 2000

- you must occupy your first home as your PPR within 12 months of construction or purchase and for a minimum of 12 continuous months.

To learn more about the stamp duty exemption policy in Victoria, head to the Victorian State Revenue Office website and search for 'stamp duty exemption'.

Table 6.6 outlines the amount of stamp duty and additional upfront costs payable as a first home buyer utilising either an exemption or concession.

**Table 6.6: first home buyer exemption/concession amounts on stamp duty in Victoria**

| Vic. home value | Stamp duty | Approx. additional upfront costs | Approx. total upfront costs |
|---|---|---|---|
| $500 000 | $0 | $2500 | $2500 |
| $600 000 | $0 | $2700 | $2700 |
| $700 000 | $24 713 | $2900 | $27 613 |
| $800 000 | $43 069 | $3100 | $46 169 |
| $900 000 | $49 069 | $3300 | $52 369 |
| $1 000 000 | $55 000 | $3500 | $58 500 |

## Queensland

The Queensland Government has recently increased the stamp duty exemption threshold from $500 000 up to $700 000. This has already helped thousands of first home buyers enter the housing market. From $700 000 to $800 000 you can claim a stamp duty concession, reducing the amount of stamp duty you pay.

To be eligible for the stamp duty exemption or concession in Queensland:

- you must be legally acquiring the property as an individual

- you must never have claimed the first home vacant land concession

- you must never have held an interest in another residence anywhere in Australia or overseas

- you must be over 18

- you must move into the home with your personal belongings and live there continually within 1 year of settlement

- you may not sell, transfer, lease or otherwise grant possession of all or part of the property in any way before you move in.

To learn more about the stamp duty exemption policy in Queensland, head to the Queensland Revenue Office website and search for 'first home concession'.

Table 6.7 outlines the amount of stamp duty and additional upfront costs payable as a first home buyer utilising either an exemption or a concession in Queensland.

**Table 6.7: first home buyer exemption/concession amounts on stamp duty in Queensland**

| QLD home value | Stamp duty | Approx. additional upfront costs | Approx. total of upfront costs |
|---|---|---|---|
| $500 000 | $0 | $3500 | $3500 |
| $600 000 | $0 | $3700 | $3700 |
| $700 000 | $0 | $3900 | $3900 |
| $800 000 | $21 850 | $4100 | $25 950 |
| $900 000 | $26 350 | $4300 | $30 650 |
| $1 000 000 | $30 850 | $4500 | $35 350 |

## Western Australia

Western Australia followed in the footsteps of Queensland, also increasing the stamp duty exemption threshold. As a first home buyer in Western Australia you can now buy a home for $450 000 or less and claim a full stamp duty exemption. Between $450 001 and $600 000 you can reduce your property tax by claiming a stamp duty concession. Unlike the FHOG, it doesn't matter whether you buy a new or established home.

To be eligible for the stamp duty exemption or concession in Western Australia:

- at least one applicant must be over 18

- you must be a first home buyer, buying as an individual, not a company or trust

- at least one applicant must be a permanent resident, Australian citizen or New Zealander holding a special category visa. New Zealand citizens must be living in Australia at the time when the eligible transaction is completed

- you must occupy your first home as your PPR within 12 months of construction or purchase and for a minimum of 6 continuous months.

To learn more about the stamp duty exemption policy in Western Australia, head to the Government of Western Australia website and search for 'first home owner duties fact sheet'.

Table 6.8 outlines the amount of stamp duty and additional upfront costs payable as a first home buyer utilising either an exemption or concession in Western Australia.

**Table 6.8: first home buyer exemption/concession amounts on stamp duty in Western Australia**

| WA home value | Stamp duty | Approx. additional upfront costs | Approx. total upfront costs |
| --- | --- | --- | --- |
| $400 000 | $0 | $1300 | $1300 |
| $500 000 | $7505 | $1500 | $9005 |
| $600 000 | $22 515 | $1700 | $24 215 |
| $700 000 | $27 265 | $1900 | $29 165 |
| $800 000 | $32 871 | $2100 | $34 971 |
| $900 000 | $37 465 | $2300 | $39 765 |

## South Australia

South Australia has made the greatest change to the stamp duty policy of all states and territories in Australia. Prior to 15 June 2023, South Australia had no stamp duty exemption or concession. It then implemented a stamp duty exemption for properties valued at up to $650 000. After experiencing surging house prices throughout 2024, the South Australian Government announced that from 6 June 2024 there would be no cap on the value of a home for a stamp duty exemption as long as it is a new home. This includes a house, flat, unit, townhouse or apartment, an off-the-plan apartment, a house-and-land package or vacant land to build your new home on.

To be eligible for the stamp duty exemption in South Australia:

- at least one applicant must be over 18

- you must be a first home buyer, buying as an individual, not a company or trust

- at least one applicant must be a permanent resident, Australian citizen or New Zealander holding a special category visa. New Zealand citizens must be living in Australia at the time when the eligible transaction is completed

- you must not have occupied an Australian property in which you had relevant interest for 6 months or longer

- you must not have previously received stamp duty relief for eligible first home buyers in any state or territory of Australia

- at least one applicant must occupy the home as their PPR for a continuous period of at least 6 months within

12 months of the date of settlement if buying a new home; or 12 months from the date the certificate of occupancy was used.

To learn more about the stamp duty exemption policy in South Australia head to the Revenue SA website and search for 'stamp duty relief'.

Table 6.9 outlines the amount of stamp duty and additional upfront costs payable as a first home buyer utilising an exemption when buying or building a new home vs an established home.

Table 6.9: stamp duty payable by first home buyers in South Australia, new home vs established home

| SA home value | Stamp duty on new home | Stamp duty on established home | Approx. additional upfront costs |
|---|---|---|---|
| $400 000 | $0 | $16 330 | $5000 |
| $500 000 | $0 | $21 330 | $6000 |
| $600 000 | $0 | $26 830 | $7000 |
| $700 000 | $0 | $32 080 | $8000 |
| $800 000 | $0 | $37 830 | $9000 |
| $900 000 | $0 | $43 330 | $10 000 |

## Tasmania

Just like Queensland, the Tasmanian Government has responded to increased house prices by increasing the stamp duty exemption for both new and existing homes. From 18 February 2024 until 30 June 2026 you can claim a full stamp duty exemption on properties purchased for $750 000 or less if you are a first home buyer.

To be eligible for the stamp duty exemption in Tasmania:

- at least one applicant must be over 18

- you must be a first home buyer, buying as an individual, not a company or trust

- at least one applicant must be a permanent resident, Australian citizen or New Zealander holding a special category visa. New Zealand citizens must be living in Australia at the time when the eligible transaction is completed

- you and your spouse/partner may not have ever owned or co-owned residential property in Australia

- you may not have previously received the FHOG or a stamp duty exemption or concession in any state or territory in Australia, nor may you have a spouse who has previously received the FHOG or a stamp duty exemption or concession in any state or territory in Australia.

To learn more about the stamp duty exemption policy in Tasmania, head to the State Revenue Office of Tasmania website and search for 'property transfer duties', then look for 'first home buyers of established homes duty relief'.

Table 6.10 (overleaf) outlines the amount of stamp duty and additional upfront costs payable as a first home buyer utilising either an exemption or concession in Tasmania.

Table 6.10: first home buyer exemption/concession amounts on stamp duty in Tasmania

| Tas. home value | Stamp duty | Approx. additional upfront costs | Approx. total upfront costs |
| --- | --- | --- | --- |
| $400 000 | $0 | $1300 | $1300 |
| $500 000 | $0 | $1500 | $1500 |
| $600 000 | $0 | $1700 | $1700 |
| $700 000 | $0 | $1900 | $1900 |
| $800 000 | $31 185 | $2100 | $33 285 |
| $900 000 | $35 685 | $2300 | $37 985 |

## Australian Capital Territory

Unlike the states of Australia, the ACT stamp duty exemption policy includes an income threshold component. Rather than implementing a maximum property value threshold, the ACT policy contains a maximum concession amount. In 2024–25. the maximum stamp duty concession that can be claimed is $34 270. This means that properties worth less than or equal to $1 000 000 have a payable stamp duty of $0 pending home buyer eligibility. All properties in the ACT are eligible for this scheme. It applies to vacant residential land and both new and established homes, anywhere in the ACT and at any price point.

To be eligible for the stamp duty exemption or concession in the ACT:

- all buyers of the home or land must be individuals aged at least 18
- all buyers, including their partners, must not have owned any other property in the past 5 years. A partner includes your spouse, civil union partner or de facto partner

- at least one buyer must occupy the home for a continuous period of at least 1 year, starting within 12 months of the date of completion, the settlement date or the date that the certificate of occupancy was used

- the income of all home buyers and their partners over the full financial year before the transaction date must be less than or equal to the thresholds. Your assessed taxable income will be located on the Notice of Assessment issued by the Australian Taxation Office for the financial year. Your total gross income is the sum of all earnings, including earnings other than employment income such as interest, dividends, fringe benefits, foreign income, payouts, and so on.

The 2024–25 thresholds can be found in table 6.11. They increase according to the number of children you have (up to five).

**Table 6.11: stamp duty exemption/concession income thresholds for first home buyers in the ACT**

| Number of dependent children | Total income threshold |
|---:|---:|
| 0 | $250 000 |
| 1 | $254 600 |
| 2 | $259 200 |
| 3 | $263 800 |
| 4 | $268 400 |
| 5 or more | $273 000 |

To learn more about the stamp duty exemption policy in the ACT head to the ACT Revenue Office website and search for 'home buyer concession scheme'.

Table 6.12 outlines the amount of stamp duty and additional upfront costs payable as a first home buyer utilising either an exemption or concession (pending your income threshold eligibility) in the ACT.

**Table 6.12: first home buyer exemption/concession amounts on stamp duty in the ACT pending income threshold eligibility**

| ACT home value | Stamp duty | Approx. additional upfront costs | Approx. total upfront costs |
|---|---|---|---|
| $600 000 | $0 | $1500 | $1500 |
| $700 000 | $0 | $1700 | $1700 |
| $800 000 | $0 | $1900 | $1900 |
| $900 000 | $0 | $2100 | $2100 |
| $1 000 000 | $0 | $2300 | $2300 |
| $1 100 000 | $6400 | $2500 | $8900 |

## Northern Territory

The Northern Territory has a stamp duty exemption policy similar to that of South Australia, in that only newly built properties are eligible. However, in the Northern Territory these properties must be classified as house-and-land packages.

There is no price cap for the purchased property, but the following requirements must be met to receive a full stamp duty exemption:

- The building contractor must have purchased the land from a developer who developed it as a residential lot.

- The building contractor must have paid stamp duty at the dutiable rate.

- The contract of sale must state that:

    - the building contractor will build a detached, new home on the land

    - the building contractor will finish building a partially completed new home on the land, or

    - there is a completed and detached new home on the land.

To be eligible for the house-and-land package stamp duty exemption in the Northern Territory:

- you must be over 18

- at least one applicant must be a permanent resident, Australian citizen or New Zealander holding a special category visa. New Zealand citizens must be living in Australia when the eligible transaction is completed

- you must occupy the home as your PPR within 12 months of construction or purchase and for a minimum of 6 continuous months

- you must be acquiring the whole beneficial interest in the land and you may not have had any beneficial interest in it before you bought it.

To learn more about the house-and-land package stamp duty exemption in the Northern Territory, head to the Northern Territory Government website and search for 'stamp duty exemption on house-and-land packages'.

Table 6.13 outlines the amount of stamp duty and additional upfront costs payable as a first home buyer utilising an exemption when purchasing a house-and-land package vs an established home in the Northern Territory.

**Table 6.13: stamp duty payable by first home buyers in the Northern Territory, house-and-land package vs established home**

| NT home value | Stamp duty on house-and-land package | Stamp duty on established home | Approx. additional upfront costs |
|---|---|---|---|
| $400 000 | $0 | $16 515 | $1000 |
| $500 000 | $0 | $23 929 | $1200 |
| $600 000 | $0 | $29 700 | $1400 |
| $700 000 | $0 | $34 650 | $1600 |
| $800 000 | $0 | $39 600 | $1800 |
| $900 000 | $0 | $44 550 | $2000 |

### REFLECT

## Are you eligible?

To reduce the amount of money required upfront to buy your first home, it's important to reflect on your state's or territory's eligibility criteria for schemes such as the First Home Guarantee, stamp duty exemption and First Home Owner Grant. Reflect on the following:

- Which state or territory do you intend to buy and live in?
- Are you eligible for your state's First Home Guarantee?
- If yes, what is the property value cap for your purchase location?

- What is the deposit required to purchase a home using the First Home Guarantee under your state's or territory's maximum property value (desired property value × 0.05)?
- Are you eligible for your state's or territory's stamp duty exemption or concession?
- If yes, what is the property value cap for your purchase location?
- Using the stamp duty exemption tables in this chapter, what are the total approximate upfront costs you will pay for the property you are hoping to buy?
- Are you intending to buy a newly built home or build your first home, and do you meet the eligibility for your state's or territory's FHOG?
- If yes, what is the value of your state's or territory's FHOG?
- Assuming you are eligible, approximately how much in total do you need to save to buy a home using the schemes available in your state or territory (desired property value × 0.05 + upfront costs − FHOG)?
- What is the expected value of your home loan assuming you're eligible for your state's or territory's schemes (property purchase price × 0.95)?

If you are not eligible for the First Home Guarantee, you could potentially still take advantage of a home loan allowing you to borrow up to 98 per cent LVR. In this scenario, you would need to pay LMI; however, it could be capitalised into (added to) your home loan. To calculate your savings target in this scenario multiply the desired property value by 0.05 and add your expected upfront costs. To find the expected value of your home loan, multiply the property purchase price by 0.98.

## 🏠 EXPLORE YOUR OPTIONS

## Weekly savings target

By now, you should have a fair idea of the minimum amount you need to save to buy your first home. It's probably a pretty large number. In fact, it's probably more than you've ever saved in your life. To increase the likelihood of achieving this target, we need to break it down into smaller, more achievable chunks.

You can use the following table to estimate what you'd be up for.

| What is your total savings target to buy your first home? | | | |
|---|---|---|---|
| Hit target in: | 1 year (target ÷ 52) | 2 years (target ÷ 2 ÷ 52) | 3 years (target ÷ 3 ÷ 52) |
| Per-week savings target | | | |
| Based on the maximum you can save each week, how long will it take you to hit your savings target? | | | |

The more you know, the more you'll save. With schemes such as the FHBG only available through certain banks, it can be a significant benefit to use a mortgage broker when buying your first home. They will be able to create a home-buying plan specific to your situation that takes advantage of all possible schemes. They will also be able to discuss the option of a parent guarantor, or tell you whether paying for LMI might be worthwhile to escape the rental trap.

Most importantly, a mortgage broker will be able to give you direction. They will determine your maximum borrowing power and calculate exactly how much you need to save to buy your desired home. You need this savings target to create an effective budgeting strategy. Breaking your target down into achievable weekly chunks means you are more likely to make the right spending habit decision in the moment because you can easily calculate how spending that money impacts your weekly target. For example, choosing to spend $77 on dinner out seems insignificant compared to a $32 000 target, but if your weekly savings target is $154, then spending 50 per cent of this target on one dinner becomes much harder to digest.

## CASE STUDY

## Victor and Priya's home-buying journey

Victor and Priya sold their first home back in 2018 to fund a 12-month adventure around the world. While travelling, they fell in love with Vancouver, Canada and decided to apply for a working visa. In 2023, Victor and Priya, at the ages of 40 and 36 respectively, moved back to their home city of Adelaide. Their goal was to re-enter the housing market as soon as possible. To minimise their living expenses, they moved in with Priya's parents rent-free. While overseas, Victor and Priya saved $30 000, and they had set their sights on buying a home close to Priya's parents' home.

*(continued)*

## Victor and Priya's financial snapshot

| | | | |
|---|---|---|---|
| Victor's annual before-tax income | $100 000 | Parent guarantor | No |
| Priya's annual before-tax income | $90 000 | Monthly living expenses | $1500 |
| Total annual before-tax income | $190 000 | Total credit card limits | $0 |
| Job titles | Victor: Engineer Priya: Accountant | Monthly personal loan repayments | $0 |
| Total savings | $95 000 | Monthly student debt repayments | $834 |
| Eligible for government support | No: they are not first home buyers | Residency status | Australian citizens |

## Victor and Priya's outcome

Since Priya's parents were kind enough to let them live with them rent-free, Victor and Priya were able to save a combined total of $1250 per week. After only 12 months, they had saved $65 000. With the $30 000 they already had in savings, Victor and Priya now had $95 000 to contribute towards their house purchase.

The only aspect of their financial situation that impacted their borrowing power was their student loans. (They were not required to make any payments towards these debts during the 5 years they were living in Canada.) Despite this, they still had a maximum borrowing power of $846 000.

They found a five-bedroom, two-bathroom house a few streets away from Priya's parents' house and purchased the home for $800000. In total, they were charged just over $45000 in upfront costs, mainly due to stamp duty. This left them with $50000 to contribute towards the loan. Since they both weren't first home buyers and didn't have access to a parent guarantor, Victor and Priya borrowed 98 per cent of the home's value, as well as LMI. They ended up with a home loan of $784000 and repayments of $1144 per week.

# Key takeaways for your home-buying journey

- To buy your first home you will need to save enough money to contribute a deposit as well as pay for your upfront costs, which include stamp duty, land office administration fees, agent's fees and conveyancing.

- If you contribute less than a 20 per cent deposit, your bank will charge you a one-off premium for an LMI policy. This protects the bank from incurring a loss in the event they need to sell your home after you have taken possession — for example, if you default on your loan repayments. The policy does not protect you, the home buyer, in any way.

- To avoid being charged LMI, you can apply for the First Home Guarantee, where the government guarantees up to 15 per cent of your property purchase. You need to check the eligibility criteria as well as the maximum property value caps for your state or territory.

- If you live in a regional area, you can apply for the Regional Home Guarantee. This scheme mirrors the First Home Guarantee by requiring a 5 per cent deposit with no LMI, but is designed for first home-buyers living in regional areas.

- As a single parent, you could potentially utilise the Family Home Guarantee. The government will guarantee up to 18 per cent of your property purchase price, meaning you only need a 2 per cent deposit. It's important to check eligibility criteria to see that you meet the requirements of a 'single parent'.

- Shared equity schemes, such as the Victorian Home Buyer Fund, involve the government buying a portion of your home. This is designed to help first home buyers with limited borrowing power to enter the housing market. You have to ask for government approval if you want to renovate and your financial situation will be reviewed annually.

- If your parents are willing to become your guarantors, you could potentially buy a home with no savings in the bank. They will need enough equity in their home to cover your 20 per cent deposit as well as your upfront costs up to 80 per cent of the value of their home.

- As a first home buyer it's likely you'll be able to claim a stamp duty exemption as long as you're eligible for your state's or territory's scheme and you're buying a property under that state's or territory's maximum property value cap.

- To enter the housing market as soon as possible it's important to calculate the total amount you need in savings and create a weekly savings target. You'll increase the likelihood of reaching your overall target by consistently budgeting.

- To determine your maximum borrowing power and calculate exactly how much you need to save, completely free of charge, get connected to Australian mortgage brokers via my website: *www.trustedfinance.loans*

# 7 | What should you LOOK FOR in a HOME LOAN?

There are two types of housing market: a buyer's market and a seller's market. In a buyer's market there's less demand for houses than there are properties for sale. This puts the buyer in the power position. In a seller's market, there are fewer properties for sale than there are people who want to buy them. This puts the seller in the power position. Since 2020, housing prices across Australia have increased consistently. Each city has experienced different growth rates depending on the number of houses for sale vs buyer demand.

In July 2024, as I write this, Perth is experiencing a strong seller's market. To put it into perspective, according to the *reiwa* website, there are currently 2793 properties listed for sale and the median selling time is only 8 days. In July 2023 there were 3753 properties for sale with a median selling time of 11 days, and back in 2019 there were 11 222 properties for sale in Perth with a median selling time of 58 days. In other words, in July 2019 there were four times more properties for sale and they took more than seven times longer to sell compared to July 2023. In that same five-year period, Perth has grown in population by approximately 127 000 people. That's a 6.3 per cent increase in population against a 75 per cent decrease in properties listed for sale. This concoction of population growth and listing decline has created the ultimate seller's market.

Let me tell you about Liam, whom I met a few months ago. He had already put offers on seven different homes. Each of his offers was rejected. Liam's level of frustration grew after each rejection. He thought it was as simple as offering the most amount of money — which, in some cases, it is. But the selling agent and the sellers themselves take into consideration many other factors as well. Have you already organised your finance? Can you prove it? In today's property market in Perth, most real estate agents are fielding several offers to buy a home, only presenting the most competitive offers to the seller.

Before you waste your time looking for a home and risk becoming completely demoralised by the process, you need to secure a home loan preapproval.

## Securing a preapproval

Preapproval is another way of saying that a bank has 'conditionally' approved you for a home loan. It shows the seller that a bank will approve your home loan based on your income vs your expenses and liabilities. The bank will classify your preapproval as 'conditional' because they will need to review the property you plan to purchase before transitioning your 'conditional' approval to 'unconditional'.

To secure a preapproval, it's best to reach out to a mortgage broker. After an initial chat, they will ask you to complete a 'fact find'. This is usually in the form of a link emailed to the home buyer, prompting them to answer questions about their income, expenses, liabilities and assets. In Australia, mortgage brokers are bound by a policy known as the 'best interest duty'. This policy ensures that they act in your best interest, finding you the home loan product best suited to your needs. It's in this 'fact find' that you can detail your property goals and list what you value in a bank as well as in a home loan.

Once the mortgage broker has received your fact find information, they will organise a time to have a more detailed discussion about your goals, calculate your maximum borrowing power and reveal the type of home you could potentially buy. This meeting will give you an opportunity to ask questions. Remember, this process isn't about getting the maximum possible borrowing power—it's about buying a home you can afford. Once you've been presented with your maximum borrowing power, don't be afraid to ask questions like:

- Am I eligible for any first home buyer schemes?
- Am I eligible for a stamp duty exemption?
- What will my monthly repayments on a home loan of this size be?
- If interest rates were to increase by 1 per cent, what would my new monthly repayments be?
- If I were to find a home $100 000 cheaper than my maximum borrowing power, what would my repayments be?

The next step is for your mortgage broker to prepare a home loan options report. In this report, they will present several home loan options across a range of banks. Their goal is to find a home loan product that adheres to your list of desired features, provides the lowest interest rate and gives you the funds required to buy the home of your choice. Once you've selected your preferred home loan product, the mortgage broker will apply to the bank on your behalf. Upon being successfully reviewed by the bank, you will receive your conditional approval. You can ask your mortgage broker to provide you with a letter confirming that you have secured a preapproval to help strengthen your home buying offers.

# Interest rates

Interest rates are one of the most important considerations when you're shopping for a home loan. It definitely pays to compare rates and secure the lowest rate you can.

## Comparing interest rates

Unless you do the numbers, it's hard to determine the impact of an interest rate difference. For example, how much money could you possibly save on an interest rate of 6.2 per cent compared to 6.8 per cent? After all, there's only 0.6 per cent difference!

I've met countless home buyers trapped by this mindset: willing to settle on an interest rate because a difference of, say, 0.6 per cent seems insignificant. Don't be one of them. In table 7.1 I'll show you why.

Table 7.1 compares the interest paid on a $600 000 home loan based on an annual interest rate of 6.2 per cent and 6.8 per cent.

**Table 7.1: difference in interest paid over 30 years at 6.2% and 6.8%***

| Home loan of $600 000 | Monthly repayments | Interest paid after 1 year | Interest paid after 15 years | Interest paid after 30 years |
| --- | --- | --- | --- | --- |
| 6.2% p.a. | $3675 | $36 391 | $490 000 | $722 933 |
| 6.8% p.a. | $3912 | $40 112 | $543 392 | $808 159 |
| **Difference** | **$237** | **$3721** | **$53 392** | **$85 226** |

*Assuming the variable interest rate remains constant for the full term of the home loan.

As you can see, a difference in interest rate of only 0.6 per cent means the home buyer securing a $600 000 mortgage pays $85 226 less in interest over a 30-year term. In my opinion, the difference in repayments is the most compelling figure. At $237 less per month, that's potentially $2844 extra in savings over 1 year if your rate is 6.2 per cent compared to someone with an identical outstanding mortgage on a rate of 6.8 per cent. What would this money do for your mental health? Would you add it to your emergency savings fund account? Would you spend it on a holiday? Does it mean you can pay for your kids' after-school sporting commitments?

At the start of 2020, I had finally taken control of my income. My wife and I were at a point financially where we could comfortably meet the mortgage repayments of our variable interest home loan. Then the COVID pandemic devastated the world. Our household income reduced by 90 per cent overnight with the Western Australian Government–imposed lockdown restrictions forcing us to close our small business. By the end of 2020, we were back on our feet and our business had recovered, but the sting remained. The feeling of helplessness. The lack of control.

At the start of 2021, one of the four major banks announced they were increasing their 4-year fixed interest rates. It was the first time any of the four major banks had increased their fixed interest rates in years. (We'll look at the difference between variable and fixed rates in the next section.) This action indicated that rate rises were on the horizon. At this point in time, the Reserve Bank of Australia (RBA) had set the cash rate at an all-time low of 0.1 per cent.

Despite the RBA's stand-still at 0.1 per cent, I decided to act. I transitioned my variable interest rate of 1.78 per cent to an interest rate of 1.98 per cent fixed for 4 years. Retrospectively it seems like a no-brainer, but at the time, there were few people willing to lock in a fixed rate above the best variable rate they could find. But I wanted security. I wanted control over my repayments. My goal in 2021 was to start a new business and I needed to know exactly how much I'd be paying towards my mortgage each month. This gave me more than peace of mind—it gave me the confidence to risk starting a new business in a completely different industry. That business, Trusted Finance, has grown beyond my wildest dreams and led me to writing the book you're reading right now. So how much did I save in interest on my home loan?

As at July 2024, the best interest rate my bank offers is 6.19 per cent variable. My current interest rate is still 1.98 per cent, fixed until

March of 2025. Let's examine the difference in repayments between these two interest rates on a mortgage of $800 000 (see table 7.2).

**Table 7.2: difference in monthly repayments between 6.19% and 1.98% interest rates on a home loan of $800 000**

| Home loan of $800 000 | Monthly repayments |
|---|---|
| 6.19% p.a. | $4895 |
| 1.98% p.a. | $2949 |
| Difference | $1946 |

This monthly difference in repayments is mind blowing. By securing a 4-year fixed interest rate at 1.98 per cent back in 2021, I'm paying $23 352 less per year in repayments than someone on a highly competitive variable interest rate of 6.19 per cent in 2024.

It's important to note, that while this might have been the case over the past 4 years, the next 4 years could be completely different. Australia's top economic forecasters expect the RBA to start cutting interest rates in 2025. They predict that the cash rate will fall from 4.35 per cent to 3.75 per cent by the end of 2025. If their prediction is correct, fixing an interest rate now would mean you miss out on the reduction in repayments moving forward.

## Variable or fixed?

When you choose a home loan, you can elect for the interest rate to be variable or fixed.

If you're on a variable rate, the rate will go up or down at the bank's discretion. The RBA is responsible for setting the official cash rate and raises or lowers this on a regular basis. The RBA's cash rate fluctuations influence whether banks increase or decrease their variable home loan interest rates.

With fixed interest rates, you are securing an interest rate for a certain period. Most banks offer 1-year, 2-year, 3-year, 4-year and 5-year fixed rates.

So which one's the better option? If only we had a crystal ball to see into the future. Table 7.3 looks at pros and cons of variable vs fixed interest rates.

**Table 7.3: pros and cons of variable and fixed interest rates**

| Variable interest rate | |
|---|---|
| **Pros** | **Cons** |
| ▪ If interest rates decrease you will end up paying less interest on your home loan. This will reduce your minimum monthly repayment. | ▪ If interest rates rise, you will pay more interest. It also means your minimum monthly repayment will increase. |
| ▪ Variable rate home loans usually offer a wide range of repayment options. For example, you may be able to pay your home loan off earlier without incurring interest rate break costs. Most also offer a redraw facility or a linked offset account feature. | ▪ As rates can change at any time, it can be difficult for you to predict cash flow over the long term. This will require financial flexibility on your part. |
| ▪ Variable rate home loans are potentially easier to refinance so it's usually easy to switch banks without attracting any break costs. | |

| Fixed interest rate | |
|---|---|
| **Pros** | **Cons** |
| • If interest rates rise within your fixed rate period, you will not be impacted. Your rate will stay the same and so will your repayments.<br>• Knowing what your repayments will be for a set time can help you budget and manage your cash flow. This will likely reduce the risk of financial stress. | • You might incur a break fee if you choose to refinance, sell or pay your loan off before the end of the fixed term period. Break costs are usually higher when interest rates fall because banks risk losing money on the difference between your fixed rate and your new variable rate.<br>• Fixed rate home loans generally do not offer features such as being able to redraw funds over the fixed period or linking an offset account.<br>• If interest rates decrease, you won't benefit from the reduced amount of interest payable or smaller home loan repayments. |

## Split loans

One way to hedge your bets on interest rates is by splitting your home loan. Many banks will give you the option of splitting your home loan into multiple accounts—for example, half fixed rate and half variable. This means you will be able to experience all the pros of a variable rate on one portion—such as linking it to an offset account—but you'll also experience the safety of consistent repayments that result from the fixed term portion.

## Finding the best interest rate

By now, you probably understand how important it is to obtain a competitive interest rate on your home loan. So how do you find the best rate?

> **EXPLORE YOUR OPTIONS**
>
> **Finding the best interest rate**
>
> There are many websites that list the best interest rates available. I like to use *Canstar*.
>
> Make sure you adjust the filter to represent your home buying situation. When comparing home loan interest rates you should use the 'comparison rate' instead of the 'interest rate'. This is because the comparison rate includes all fees and charges over the life of the loan, so it is a better representation of how much the home loan will cost you overall.
>
> Using a website like *Canstar*, find the five lowest home loan comparison rates on the market. Check the variable comparison rate as well as fixed rates for 1, 3 and 5 years.

# Home loan features

It's important to understand that a home loan is a product. In the same way as you compare the features of a TV to find the best size, display and contrast for money, different home loans contain a range of features that make them either more or less suited to your needs. Let's look at some of these features.

## *Redraw facility*

If you consistently make the minimum repayments on your home loan, your outstanding balance will match your home loan limit. Every month, your outstanding balance will decrease by the same amount as your home loan limit.

If you decide to make an extra repayment towards your home loan (on top of the required minimum repayment), then your outstanding balance will fall below your home loan limit. The difference between these two amounts is classified as surplus funds. The benefit of making extra repayments towards your home loan is that you will end up paying less interest (because you'll be paying interest on the reduced amount), which means you'll pay your home loan off faster.

Most home loans have a feature called a 'redraw facility'. This means you can easily transfer your surplus funds out of your home loan, at any time, back into either a transaction or savings account. Some banks offer this feature but charge a fee if the facility is used to redraw surplus funds, while other banks offer the feature completely free of charge.

It's a great idea to make extra repayments into your home loan. If you have a redraw facility that is completely free, then you can always transfer the money back if needed. The only downside to this equation is that you must be accountable for making the extra repayments in the first place. It's easy to become lazy and just keep the surplus funds in your transaction or savings account for when needed. This laziness is costing home owners thousands of dollars in interest. Luckily there is a more automated way to save this money on interest.

## *Offset accounts*

An offset account reduces the amount of interest you pay on your home loan. It does this by reducing the balance of your home loan on which interest is calculated. For example, if you had an outstanding home loan of $500 000 but you had $10 000 sitting in your offset account, then your bank would only be charging you interest on a home loan balance of $490 000. The restrictions around offset accounts vary from bank to bank as well as between different home loan products. Some banks only allow for one offset account per home loan and will charge a monthly fee. Others allow for one offset account included in the monthly fees of the home loan. Some banks allow for multiple offset accounts to be attached to a single home loan at no extra charge. With most banks, the biggest benefit is that a standard transaction account can also be an offset account. This means, if you were to direct your fortnightly salary and all of your savings into this offset account, you would be minimising the amount of interest charged by the bank on your home loan at all times.

Setting up your accounts can be rather confusing. Figure 7.1 illustrates how my wife and I set up ours to reduce the overall interest charged by the bank and maximise financial transparency within our relationship. This structure enabled us to pay off our home loan in 6 years.

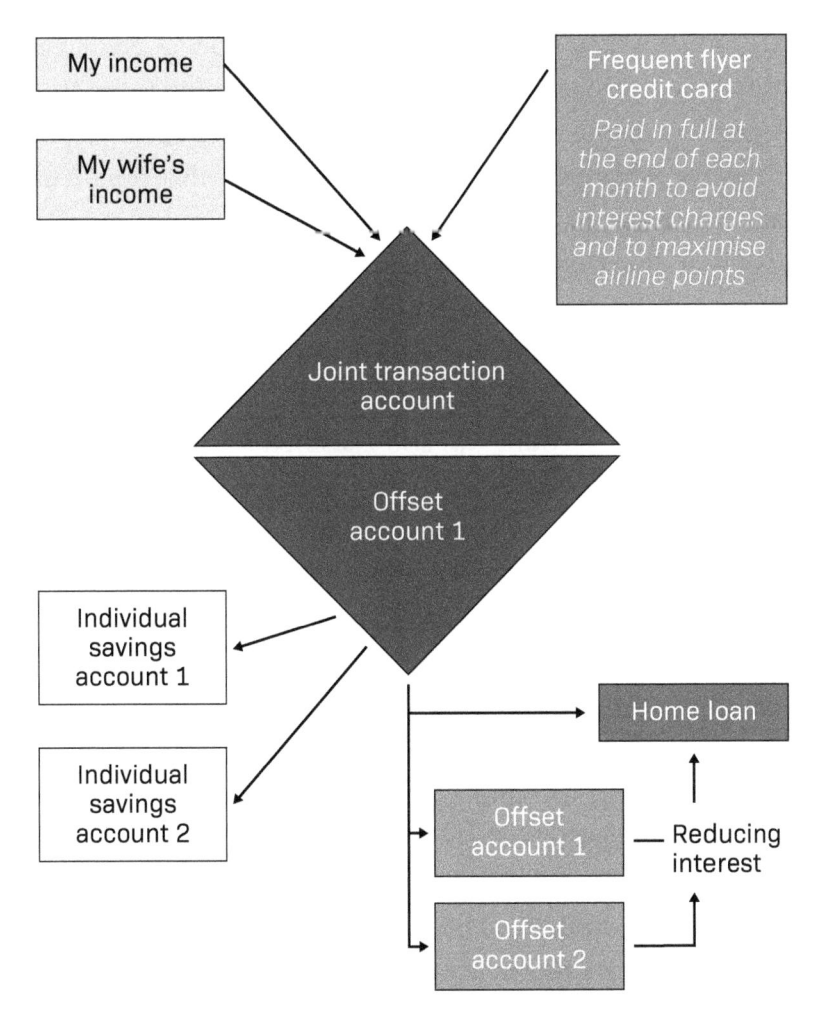

**Figure 7.1: a home loan with three offset accounts**

My wife and I earn income from a variety of sources. All these income streams were paid into our joint transaction account. We paid all our everyday living expenses from our credit card. The annual fee for our credit card was waived because our home loan package was with the same bank. We accumulate points on our credit card for every dollar we spend and have used these points to travel all over the world for a small fee compared to a full

What should you look for in a home loan? 159

price airline ticket. The problem with these types of credit cards is that they have very high interest rates if you don't pay off the full amount owing every month. I have been using a credit card for my everyday expenses for over 15 years. In that time, I have not been charged a single cent in interest. This is because I pay my outstanding balance off in full before the end of the interest-free period. The interest-free period varies depending on the credit card, so make sure you read the product disclosure guide.

Our transaction account was also classified as an offset account linked to our home loan. For years we let our savings pile up in that account, conscious of minimising the interest charged on our home loan. But, when we started creating other financial goals, we found it hard to differentiate what portion of the savings in our transaction account belonged to each of these goals. This is when we decided to activate two additional offset accounts. Offset account 2 was our travel goals account and offset account 3 was our emergency fund. We still have these accounts (though they are no longer offset accounts as we have paid off our loan) and it gives us peace of mind knowing we have an emergency fund and motivation from hitting milestones in our travel goals. While they were offset accounts they gave us the added benefit of reducing the interest on our home loan. Our home loan and our offset accounts were joint accounts in both of our names.

In addition to these accounts, we also had two separate individual savings accounts. We primarily used these accounts for buying each other birthday, anniversary or Christmas gifts. Money was only every transferred into these accounts if we intended to use it the same day. This is because your bank compounds the interest on your home loan daily. So, your goal should be to create a bank account structure that always maximises the funds in your offset accounts to minimise the daily interest compounded on your home loan.

## Construction loans

If you're planning to buy a block of land to build your first home on, you'll need to secure a construction loan. This means you're asking to borrow two portions of funds: one to pay for the land and one to fund the construction of your home based on the building contract submitted to the bank.

Construction loans are usually segmented into six portions. The first portion outstanding on your loan will represent the purchase price of the land minus your deposit. For example, if you intend to borrow $600 000 in total to buy land and build and you are buying the land for $250 000, you might have an outstanding home loan of $235 000 (at an LVR of 95%). To start with, you will only make repayments on this portion. To make it even more manageable, as most people are also paying rent during the construction process, most banks will allow you to make interest only (IO) payments. To put this into perspective, on a $235 000 loan at, say, 6.3 per cent per annum, you would usually pay $1455 per month in principal and interest repayments. With an 'interest only' loan you would only pay $1234 per month.

The split of the remaining portions of your home loan will be determined by your building contract. Most builders ask for five progress payments to be made over the duration of the build. These are payable at various stages, which will be outlined in your contract. Many builders expect the first payment to be made after the flooring has been constructed. At each stage of construction you should review your builder's work before agreeing to release a progress payment.

You will be notified at each stage of completion and your bank will request your permission to release each progress payment to the builder. For example, say the first progress payment is for $75 000. After you have agreed, the bank will transfer this amount to the builder, and your outstanding home loan balance will increase from $235 000 to $310 000. Your monthly IO repayments will also be adjusted from $1234 to $1628. Once your home is fully constructed and the final progress payment has been made, the outstanding balance on your mortgage will be the land cost plus the build cost minus your deposit—in this example this would be $235 000 + $365 000 − $15 000 = $585 000. (As it's an IO loan, you won't have paid anything off the principal.)

# Non-bank lenders

The difference between banks and non-bank lenders is that banks are authorised to take deposits and offer transaction accounts in addition to offering other products such as home loans, while non-bank lenders are not deposit-taking institutions. Non-bank lenders provide credit-based products. While they are not authorised to accept customer deposits or offer products such as savings accounts and term deposits, they can provide products such as credit cards, home loans and personal loans. Even though banks still own a large majority of the mortgage market, non-bank lenders are gaining in popularity due to their competitive interest rates, fees and approval times. Table 7.4 summarises some of the advantages and disadvantages of non-bank lenders.

Table 7.4: advantages and disadvantages of non-bank lenders

| Advantages | Disadvantages |
| --- | --- |
| - Non-bank lenders usually offer faster processing times, lower fees and/or competitive interest rates.<br>- Non-bank lenders might have more flexible eligibility criteria as they have different restrictions from banks.<br>- Non-bank lenders operate on a smaller scale, potentially offering more personalised customer care. | - They cannot offer the same features as banks (e.g. offset accounts) since they do not hold an authorised deposit-taking institution licence.<br>- It's unlikely you'll be able to speak to someone face to face if the non-bank lender is mainly digital or online.<br>- You will have your banking needs split across institutions if you want other products, such as savings accounts or term deposits. |

# Paying off your home loan

Hopefully this chapter has opened your eyes to everything you need to look for in a home loan. While you're deciding which one is right for you, there's one more thing you need to reflect on: will you be able to afford the repayments?

### REFLECT

### Can you afford the repayments?

Before you commit to a home loan, it's important to reflect on its affordability. Can you afford the variable interest rate repayments now? What if interest rates increase by 1 per cent? What will the repayments be if you lock in your interest rate for a few years?

*(continued)*

You can calculate what you'll be paying each month by using an online repayment calculator. I like the one on the Commonwealth Bank's website (search for 'mortgage repayment calculator'). You might like to use a table like this one to record and compare the results. I've given you an example.

| What is the expected size of your home loan? | $570 000 | |
|---|---|---|
| **Type of loan** | **Interest rate p.a.** | **Monthly repayment** |
| Variable rate | 6.3% | $3529 |
| Variable rate + 1% | 7.3% | $3908 |
| Variable rate + 2% | 8.3% | $4303 |
| Fixed rate: 1 year | 6.74% | $3694 |
| Fixed rate: 3 years | 6.64% | $3656 |
| Fixed rate: 5 years | 6.89% | $3751 |

Finding the right home loan for your needs is imperative. While the interest rate is important, there are also other factors that impact whether a home loan is right for you. You might need to choose a lender that is more flexible in its eligibility requirements to borrow enough to buy your desired home. You might plan to structure your accounts in a way that requires your home loan to have an array of features.

Trying to navigate all this information by yourself can be time consuming and overwhelming. That's why over 75 per cent of home buyers use a mortgage broker to secure their home loan instead of going directly to the bank. Get them to do the heavy lifting so you can do the house hunting.

### CASE STUDY

## Caitlin's home-buying journey

Caitlin has been working hard, building up her savings for over 3 years. At the start of 2024, just after her 29th birthday, she reached her goal of $55 000 in savings. As a registered nurse, she is earning a healthy income of $105 000 before tax per year. As a first home buyer she is eligible for the First Home Guarantee and the ACT's stamp duty exemption. Caitlin had her sights set on buying a three-bedroom apartment in Canberra, but every offer she's made has been rejected. After a total of nine rejections, Caitlin decided to adjust her expectations.

### Caitlin's financial snapshot

| | | | |
|---|---|---|---|
| **Annual before-tax income** | $105 000 | **Monthly living expenses** | $2000 |
| **Job title** | Nurse | **Total credit card limits** | $0 |
| **Total savings** | $55 000 | **Monthly personal loan repayments** | $0 |
| **Eligible for government support** | Yes: FHBG and stamp duty exemption | **Monthly student debt repayments** | $525 |
| **Parent guarantor** | No | **Residency status** | Australian citizen |

### Caitlin's outcome

The only liability that negatively impacts Caitlin's maximum borrowing power is her student loan. With this taken into account, her borrowing power is $460 000. All the apartments Caitlin made an offer to buy had price guides

*(continued)*

starting at $460 000. Since she needed to retain some savings to furnish the property, the maximum offer she could make was $480 000. In the current market, her offers were not competitive enough.

Instead, Caitlin adjusted her expectations and started looking at two-bedroom apartments, with price guides starting at $440 000. She found multiple apartments with better layouts, amenities and locations than the three-bedroom properties she'd viewed previously. She made her best possible offer of $480 000 and secured a two-bedroom, one-bathroom apartment only minutes from her work.

Caitlin now has a $456 000 home loan (at an LVR of 95 per cent) and her repayments are $666 per week. She also has to pay approximately $110 per week in strata fees (also known as body corporate fees — I'll explain what these are in chapter 8).

# Key takeaways for your home-buying journey

- In a seller's market, there are fewer houses for sale than people who want to buy them. In a buyer's market, there are more houses for sale than people who want to buy them. Most Australian cities have been in a seller's market since 2020.

- To strengthen your home-buying offer, it's important to organise your finance first. Reach out to a mortgage broker to secure a preapproval so you know exactly how much you can offer on a property. Head to *Trusted Finance* online to be connected with high-quality mortgage brokers Australia-wide.

- A variable home loan interest rate can increase or decrease at the bank's discretion, directly impacting your monthly repayments. A fixed interest rate locks your rate in for a certain period. This means your monthly repayments will also remain constant. Fixed interest rate home loans usually result in fewer home loan features such as offset accounts.

- An offset account is a type of transaction or savings account that can be linked to your home loan. The amount in your offset account will reduce your outstanding home loan balance, which means your interest is reduced.

- A redraw facility enables you to transfer any surplus funds from your home loan to your transaction or savings account. This feature gives you peace of mind because you know that any extra repayments made to your home loan can be withdrawn.

- Construction loans are usually segmented into six portions: the initial loan for the land followed by five progress payments to the builder. As each progress payment is made, your home loan increases in size until it is 'fully drawn', which is when you receive the keys to your new home.

- Non-bank lenders offer home loans and other credit-based products. They're usually competitive on rate and have reduced application time frames. Since they are not authorised deposit-taking institutions, their home loans usually don't contain features such as offset accounts.

# 8 | What TYPE of HOME SHOULD you BUY?

When my wife and I bought our first home, we were double income no kids (DINKS). We were both working fulltime, splitting the cost of life. Just like so many other DINKS, this reality lulled us into a false sense of security. It's hard to anticipate what life is going to be like once you have kids.

The first change is obvious: one of you will need to work less. For most people, working less will result in less income. Even if you both end up working fulltime, most parents will need to pay for day care. Unless one or both of you experience a substantial pay increase, the result is reduced household cash flow.

It's the other aspects of parenthood that caught me off guard. We had less time for ourselves, less time for each other and our energy levels were at an all-time low. The word 'depleted' comes to mind, but it feels like an understatement.

You might be wondering how parenthood relates to buying your first home. Well, imagine if you felt depleted and then added to that a suffocating dose of mortgage stress. Stress, just like the interest on your mortgage, has a habit of compounding daily. So, before you consider what type of home you should buy you need to figure out how much you can spend. And before you can calculate how much to spend you need to ask yourself the following questions.

1. Have you reached an income ceiling based on your profession or will it continue to grow?

2. If you are in a DINK relationship, do both of you need to continue working fulltime to afford the home you intend to buy?

3. If you are in a DINK relationship, where do you think you'll be in 5 years? Have you discussed how many kids you'd like to have? Have you decided who the primary caregiver will be?

4. How long do you think you'll live in your first home? Can your family grow in this home?

I've met many people forced to sell their first home after realising they could no longer afford it as new parents. Some were able to use the profit they made from selling it to buy a more modest house for their second purchase. Others weren't so lucky. After realtor fees, these people sold their home with very little to show for it, and were forced back into the rental market. And re-entering the housing market has just became so much harder for them because they're no longer eligible for first home buyer schemes such as the First Home Buyer Guarantee, they can't access the First Home Owner Grant and they will have to pay the full stamp duty on any purchase. In some cases, they will need around $50 000 more in savings to buy a second home compared to how much they needed to buy their first home. I don't want you to be in this situation.

# The cost of owning a home

In chapter 6, I unveiled the upfront costs associated with buying your first home. What you might not know is that there are ongoing costs—also known as hidden costs—in addition to your mortgage repayments that many first home buyers don't allow for in their budget. The reason why you may not have considered these costs is because they are paid for by your landlord when you are renting.

So, it's time to look at the ongoing costs of owning a home.

## *Council rates*

As a home owner you will need to pay annual rates to your local council. This money is used for a variety of initiatives, depending on your city or shire, but is often utilised to pay for waste services, parks and suburb maintenance. Each city calculates rates differently; however, most base the amount on the gross rental value of your property.

This is the annual rental income you could expect to receive from renting out your home. The gross rental value is then multiplied by a predetermined dollar rate to calculate an annual fee. For example, in my city, the rate in the dollar is 6.68 cents. So, for a home with a gross rental value of $36 000 per year, the annual rates would be 36 000 multiplied by 0.068, totalling $2448 per year or $204 per month.

Most local councils will give you the option to pay your rates in 3-month, 6-month or 12-month instalments. As the gross rental value increases over time, so will your annual rates.

## *Water rates*

As a renter, you are only responsible for paying your water usage charges. The water service fee, drainage charges and sewage charges—also known as the water rates—are paid by the home owner. This fee can vary depending on the type of property you buy. For example, a home connected to sewage could incur a higher service fee than one that has septic tanks. In most states the sewage fee is calculated similarly to the council rates, by multiplying the rate by the gross rental value. For a home with a gross rental value of $36 000 you could expect to pay around $1600 a year, or $133 per month. This doesn't include the water usage charges.

## *Insurance*

When renting, you might opt to take out a contents insurance policy. However, it is the landlord's responsibility to insure the building. This is another cost usually not considered by home buyers. When applying for a home loan, your bank may require the 'certificate of currency' as evidence they have been listed as the mortgagee. This insurance premium will vary based on the provider, type of home and sum insured. One insurance provider recently quoted me $154 a month for a brick home, built in 1988, to be insured for $300 000 with an excess of $750. Make sure you get a building insurance quote to budget for this cost before making an offer on a property.

## *Maintenance*

There are lots of variables involved when trying to calculate the expected annual maintenance costs of a property. An older property will need more money spent on maintenance than a newer property. However, a property with a smaller yard will require much less spent on maintaining the yard. My block is over 4000 m² in size and full of large trees. To keep our property safe and in line with our city's bush fire management policies, we spend between $5000 and $10 000 per year in tree lopping. When calculating a realistic number for your property, many home buyers use the 1-per-cent rule. Calculate 1 per cent of the property value and divide this by 12. This is your average monthly maintenance cost. For example, on a $600 000 property, it would be $500 per month.

## *Body corporate fees*

Body corporate fees, also known as strata fees, are usually payable quarterly when you buy a townhouse, unit or apartment. These fees are paid by all of the home owners in the complex and are used for maintaining common areas. A complex with more amenities—such as pools, gyms and saunas—generally charges higher strata fees; however, that's not always the case. Recently, a friend of mine was trying to buy an apartment in Perth. He was looking for a two-bedroom, two-bathroom apartment for under $500 000 less than 10 minutes from the CBD. He found two apartments just down the road from each other. Perth apartments are comparable in size and layout. The complex that contained a pool, sauna, communal barbeque area and communal patio area charged $1100 per quarter, or $367 per month. The complex without these amenities charged $1540 per quarter, or $513 per month because it was a newer building. Don't be afraid to ask the selling real estate agent for minutes from the last body corporate meeting. These will give you insight into how the strata fees are distributed and help you decide if you're happy spending money on maintaining those features of your complex.

> ### REFLECT
>
> ## Can you afford the hidden costs?
>
> In chapter 7, you reflected on your potential mortgage repayments. But in addition to these repayments, you must also be able to afford the hidden costs. Here's a checklist to help you figure out if you can afford the repayments as well as the hidden costs.
>
> - What is the expected size of your home loan?
> - What will the monthly repayments of your home loan be?
> - What are the monthly council rates of a home of this value in this suburb?
> - What are the expected monthly water rates for a home of this value in this suburb?
> - What is the expected monthly building insurance cost for a home of this value?
> - What is the expected monthly maintenance cost for a home of this value?

- Are you planning to buy a townhouse, unit or apartment with body corporate or strata fees attached? If so, what is the monthly cost of these?
- What is your total monthly cost to own this home?
- What percentage of your after-tax household income is being spent on the total cost to own this home (total monthly cost of owning home ÷ total monthly household income × 100)?
- Is your total household income based on two incomes? If so, are you planning to have children in the future? How would this affect your income?
- What percentage of your expected after-tax household income will be spent on the total cost of owning this home (total monthly cost of owning home ÷ total expected monthly household income × 100)?

# How much can you afford to pay?

In some cities across Australia, you could expect to be able to buy a house for your first home. These cities are still affordable. In a city such as Sydney, most home buyers are aiming to enter the market by purchasing a townhouse, unit or apartment.

## *Houses*

Houses are still the most popular type of dwelling purchase for first home buyers in Australia. When buying a house, you are also purchasing the land on an individual title. Being that this type of dwelling is the most popular, it also attracts the highest price tag, especially closer to the capital city CBDs.

See table 8.1 (overleaf) for some pros and cons of owning a house.

**Table 8.1: pros and cons of owning a house**

| Pros | Cons |
| --- | --- |
| *More space* It's more likely that a house will be a dwelling you can grow into as a family. Most houses also have either a front yard, backyard or both. | *Cost* Houses tend to be more expensive than other dwellings in a similar location. |
| *Privacy* Houses offer greater privacy as they do not share common spaces. | *Maintenance* The bigger the dwelling, the more you'll probably spend maintaining it. The added space of a front yard, backyard or both also increases your maintenance costs. |
| *Resale value* In general, houses appreciate more than townhouses, units or apartments. | *More expensive bills* Houses are usually bigger and therefore cost more to heat and cool. |

## Townhouses

A townhouse is a multi-level building designed to contain most of the features of a traditional house. However, it is owned on a strata title. This means you own the dwelling but share the land with other people. They may have a body corporate and require you to pay strata fees.

See table 8.2 for some pros and cons of owning a townhouse.

**Table 8.2: pros and cons of owning a townhouse**

| Pros | Cons |
| --- | --- |
| *Modern amenities* Townhouses are likely to include modern amenities such as ensuites and open-plan floorplans. | *Shared title* You are on a strata scheme and therefore only own part of the land. |

| Pros | Cons |
|---|---|
| *Price* <br> Compared to houses, townhouses are much more affordable for a similar amount of living space. | *Stairs* <br> Townhouses typically span two or three storeys, which might not suit home buyers with mobility issues. |
| *Location* <br> You're more likely to find a townhouse in a competitive location, such as near the city or beach, due to the large number of townhouse developments in popular locations. | *Resale value* <br> Townhouses usually experience less capital growth than houses. |

## *Units*

Units may include either a standalone house or an attached dwelling on land that has been subdivided. Often, these properties share driveways, parking areas and other outdoor spaces and could be attached to an owners corporation, requiring fees similar to strata fees.

Table 8.3 lists some pros and cons of living in a unit.

**Table 8.3: pros and cons of living in a unit**

| Pros | Cons |
|---|---|
| *Dwelling type* <br> As opposed to townhouses, some units are standalone and don't share any walls with neighbouring properties. | *Land size* <br> Compared to a house, the land size of a unit will be substantially smaller. |
| *Alterations* <br> Owners can make changes to their dwelling as they would a standalone house, as long as it's not part of the shared or common space, unlike owners of a strata title. | *Price* <br> Compared to a townhouse, units generally attract a higher price due to owning a larger parcel of land. |

*(continued)*

**Table 8.3: pros and cons of living in a unit (*cont'd*)**

| Pros | Cons |
|---|---|
| *Outdoor spaces* <br> Units usually have either a front yard, backyard or smaller version of both depending on where the unit is located on a subdivided block. | *Older features* <br> Many units on the market are older compared to townhouses and have more outdated floorplans. |

## Apartments

An apartment is a self-contained flat that is part of a bigger complex. Owning an apartment will mean you belong to a body corporate and must comply with certain requirements. You will also need to pay body corporate fees to cover the repair and maintenance of common areas. The amount you pay depends on the apartment size, the number of apartments within the complex, the age of the complex and its amenities. See table 8.4 for a few pros and cons of owning an apartment.

**Table 8.4: pros and cons of owning an apartment**

| Pros | Cons |
|---|---|
| *Affordability* <br> Apartments are the most affordable type of dwelling for a first home buyer. | *Common walls* <br> Depending on your apartment's location within the complex, you might share common walls or ceilings with multiple properties. |
| *Location* <br> Apartments give first home buyers on a cheaper budget the opportunity to live in better locations. | *Reduced flexibility* <br> Depending on your body corporate bylaws, there might be stipulations around pets, noise levels, where you can hang your washing and whether you can renovate. |
| *Amenities* <br> Many apartments come with added extras such as communal pools, gyms, saunas and lifts. | *Parking* <br> Increased competition for car spaces in apartment complexes can impact the price of having an individual space on your title. |

# What's the best location?

Location is one of the biggest influences on dwelling price. In major cities, closeness to the CBD or coast tend to drastically increase prices. Many home buyers experience living in these locations when renting, only to realise that buying a home there is unaffordable. House prices have climbed so dramatically over the past 4 years, that even the outer suburbs are becoming unaffordable. Currently in Sydney, for example, even a three-bedroom, one-bathroom house built in the 1970s that is more than a 45-minute drive from the CBD is selling for more than $700 000.

If you've been priced out of your city, it's worth considering moving to a regional or interstate location to buy your first home. This may mean uprooting your current life and finding new employment (or working remotely) but it will give you the opportunity to enter the housing market. You may then be able to leverage the capital growth of this property to buy your next property in the city of your choice.

## *Moving to a regional area*

Naturally, being able to drive back to your home city for the weekend would make leaving your friends and family to move to a regional area easier to consider. But this isn't always possible. Some regional locations in Western Australia and Queensland, for example, are thousands of kilometres away from their state's capital. On the positive side, there are usually benefits employment-wise for moving to regional areas that are facing staff shortages.

If you're deciding whether to move to a regional area for more affordable home purchase prices, start by researching different regional areas in your state. Often, a simple Google search will yield some results, but you could make it more specific by using an employment search engine to find job opportunities in regional areas.

## *Moving interstate*

In most cases, a different state will have a completely different property market from that of your home city. It could be much cheaper, or far more expensive, depending on where you currently live. As I am writing this, in July of 2024, Sydney is still the most expensive city in Australia, followed by Canberra. However, Brisbane has recently moved into third place, with last quarter's results showing a higher median dwelling price than Melbourne. The house prices of these four cities are prompting first home buyers to look elsewhere.

The most popular choice at the moment is Perth. Perth's recent population surge has propelled home prices, but they are still cheaper than those of the eastern states. Many home buyers I've spoken to who have moved to Western Australia from the eastern states say it's the best decision they've ever made. A large proportion of these home buyers have drastically increased their income by securing a job in the mining industry, entered the property market at a lower price than they could have back in their home city and are enjoying a life of minimised mortgage stress. Moving interstate isn't for everyone, but if you're one of the people trapped in the rental market because your city has become unaffordable, then it's worth doing some research.

## 🏠 EXPLORE YOUR OPTIONS

# Dwelling types and locations

In chapter 1, you explored dwellings across a range of cities in Australia. By now you should have clear income goals, understand your maximum borrowing power and have calculated both your upfront costs and the ongoing costs of owning a home. You should understand the differences between dwelling types and be able to research employment opportunities in different locations across Australia.

If you haven't yet decided where to buy and/or what type of home to buy, it might be time to put all of these skills into practice by doing some meaningful research. Here's a template you can use to help you decide if moving regionally or interstate is an option for you.

| Regional town in your state | | | |
|---|---|---|---|
| **House** | **Townhouse** | **Unit** | **Apartment** |
| Suburb: | Suburb: | Suburb: | Suburb: |
| Beds: | Beds: | Beds: | Beds: |
| Baths: | Baths: | Baths: | Baths: |
| Other features: | Other features: | Other features: | Other features: |
| Price: | Price: | Price: | Price: |
| **Interstate city** | | | |
| Suburb: | Suburb: | Suburb: | Suburb: |
| Beds: | Beds: | Beds: | Beds: |
| Baths: | Baths: | Baths: | Baths: |
| Other features: | Other features: | Other features: | Other features: |
| Price: | Price: | Price: | Price: |

*(continued)*

| Interstate regional town | | | |
|---|---|---|---|
| Suburb: | Suburb: | Suburb: | Suburb: |
| Beds: | Beds: | Beds: | Beds: |
| Baths: | Baths: | Baths: | Baths: |
| Other features: | Other features: | Other features: | Other features: |
| Price: | Price: | Price: | Price: |

# Rentvesting

A growing number of first home buyers in Australia are choosing to rent where they want to live and buy where they can afford. This is known as rentvesting. Most home buyers choosing this pathway are renting in an unaffordable city like Sydney and buying in a more affordable location like Perth, where they then rent out their property. For those of you who are not willing to relocate, this strategy has its positives. However, by becoming an investor, you forgo most of your first home buyer benefits. The rentvestors willing to make this sacrifice are betting on gaining more from the capital growth of their investment than from the loss of their first home buyer benefits. Often, they have rationalised this decision by succumbing to the realisation that they can't afford to buy a home in their city anyway. See table 8.5 for a few pros and cons of rentvesting.

**Table 8.5: pros and cons of rentvesting**

| Pros | Cons |
|---|---|
| *Friends, family and career* <br> You can continue renting near your friends and family in the city that you love while also building your career with your current employer. | *Subjected to rental market* <br> You will continue to experience all the negatives that come with renting, such as rental inspections, rent increases and termination of rental leases. |
| *Capital growth* <br> Buying in a more affordable location interstate increases the likelihood that you could buy a house rather than an apartment, thereby maximising capital growth. | *Forgo first home buyer benefits* <br> You are only eligible for the First Home Guarantee, First Home Owner Grant and stamp duty exemption if you live in the property. |
| *Rental income* <br> Since you're buying an investment property, you will be receiving a rental income. You could buy in a location focused on a high rental yield to maximise your cash flow. | *Increased savings required* <br> Since you will not be able to take advantage of any government incentives, it's likely you will need more in savings to purchase an investment property compared to an owner-occupied property of the same price. |
| *Increased borrowing power* <br> Depending on your rental situation, you may be able to increase your borrowing power by rentvesting as your bank will consider your expected rental income when calculating your serviceability. | *Property management fees* <br> If buying interstate, you will need a property manager to manage the property and conduct rental inspections on your behalf. You will most likely be charged a combination of fixed charges as well as an ongoing percentage of the rent you receive. |

*(continued)*

**Table 8.5: pros and cons of rentvesting (*cont'd*)**

| Pros | Cons |
|---|---|
| *Potential tax deduction* <br> The interest, rental expenses and depreciation on the property could be claimed as a tax deduction, reducing your income tax. | *The right location* <br> Buying in a regional or interstate location can be daunting. Working with a broker to find a location suited to your property goals is paramount. Head to *Trusted Finance* online to be connected with one of my investment broker referral partners. |

Choosing to rentvest if you have the option of buying an owner-occupied home is a tough decision. However, if you don't have the option of buying in your city and you're not willing to move, then getting into the housing market as soon as possible should be your goal. It's just another example of 'time in the market' over 'timing the market'.

# Making an offer

For many first home buyers, this is the most daunting part of the process. Finding a home you love then figuring out what you're happy to pay is only the beginning. You then need to negotiate with the selling real estate agent to convince the seller that your offer is worth accepting over all other offers. Follow the tips below to put forward a competitive offer without stretching yourself beyond your means.

- Get a preapproval in place from a mortgage broker. It's important to know the maximum you can offer on a home. Revealing to the real estate agent that you already have a preapproval in place will strengthen your offer.

However, it's also important not to reveal the maximum you can afford to the selling real estate agent because they may use it as ammunition to raise your offer.

- There are three main types of offer that home buyers can put on a property. The first is 'all cash'. As the saying goes, 'cash is king' and in real estate, this is definitely the case. The next strongest type of offer is 'subject to finance'. This basically means that you need to secure a home loan combined with your deposit to buy the property. Most first home buyers fall into this category. The last type of offer is 'subject to sale'. This means you must first sell a property you own before you can settle on the property you'd like to purchase. In the eyes of most sellers, this is the riskiest type of offer as it's contingent on another property selling, though it won't apply to you if you're buying your first home.

- After communicating the type of offer, you then need to outline any terms and conditions. The first I'd recommend is to make your offer subject to a building and pest inspection. This means that in the event a building and pest inspector reveals structural or pest damage, the seller must take action to rectify the issues before settlement can take place. If they are unwilling to fix the issues, you can renege on your offer. You will need to pay for the building and pest report, which could cost you anywhere between $450 and $800 depending on your location. The second term I recommend is to make your offer subject to a 'good working order' clause. This means that all gas, plumbing and electrical fittings are in good working order at the time of settlement.

- If you are making your offer subject to finance, then you will need to indicate the number of days required to secure approval from the bank. If you already have a preapproval secured, then this should be sorted in less than 10 business days. It's common for sellers to accept 28 days for finance to be approved.

- You also need to indicate how many days you need from finance approval to settlement. This period will give your conveyancer enough time to check that all documents have been received by all parties to process funds at settlement. A common time frame for settlement is 30 days from finance approval.

- In a seller's market your offer will need to be competitive. If you've received multiple rejections, then you might need to adjust your expectations. Can you look at properties selling for $50 000 less so you can put in an offer above the asking price? Persistence is the key to buying your first home.

The housing market situation in Australia has demoralised many first home buyers. I hope this chapter has opened your eyes. If you're priced out of where you currently live, you could move. If moving is off the table, then you could try rentvesting instead.

Entering the property market in Australia is challenging. More challenging than it's ever been. But it's still possible. So, buy a property in Australia while you still can.

## CASE STUDY

## Josh and Sarah's home-buying journey

Josh and Sarah, both aged 28, have been consistently saving for the past 4 years to buy a home in Sydney for themselves and their son. Unfortunately, over this time, the Sydney median house price has continued to climb, and is now sitting just above $1.4 million. Despite having a joint income of $182 000 per year before tax, their credit card debt, car loan and student loan have reduced their maximum borrowing power down to $610 000. For a while they considered buying an apartment in Sydney, but the locations they could afford were in undesirable areas.

### Josh and Sarah's financial snapshot

| | | | |
|---|---|---|---|
| Josh's annual before-tax income | $120 000 | Rent payable | $600 per week |
| Sarah's annual before-tax income | $62 000 | Monthly living expenses | $3000 |
| Total annual before-tax income | $182 000 | Total credit card limits | $7000 |
| Job titles | Josh: Electrician Sarah: Marketing consultant | Monthly personal loan repayments | $616 |
| Total savings | $75 000 | Monthly student debt repayments | $52 |
| Eligible for government support | No: Only for owner-occupied properties | Residency status | Australian citizens |

*(continued)*

## *Josh and Sarah's outcome*

Josh and Sarah decided to buy an investment property for their first home interstate, in a city they can afford, while they continued renting in Sydney. With an expected rental income of $650 per week, their maximum borrowing power was $570 000. They were unable to utilise any of the first home buyer benefits since they will not be living in the property, but their goal is to enter the property market as soon as possible to experience capital growth. They found a four-bedroom, two-bathroom house in Bunbury, Western Australia and secured the property for $580 000. Once the property goes up in value, they plan to use the equity as a deposit to buy another investment property. On a mortgage of $557 000 their repayments are $847 per week.

# Key takeaways for your home-buying journey

- If you're buying a home based on two incomes, you need to estimate whether your home will still be affordable if you start a family and your household income decreases.

- In addition to your mortgage repayments, you will need to cover ongoing costs—also known as hidden costs—such as council rates, water rates, insurance, maintenance costs and, potentially, strata fees.

- There are four types of dwelling you could buy as your first home: a house, a townhouse, an apartment or a unit.

- If you've been priced out of your city, you could investigate moving to a regional or interstate location. You could find a much more affordable home to purchase in these areas and reap the benefits of capital growth before potentially moving back to your home city.

- If moving is not an option, you could look at rentvesting instead. Rentvesting is when you rent where you love and buy where you can afford.

- Before putting an offer on a property it's important to have secured a preapproval from a mortgage broker and be clear about your terms and conditions.

- Make sure any offers you make are subject to a building and pest inspection as well as a good working order clause.

# PART III

# Get DEBT-FREE

# 9 | MANAGE your MORTGAGE

It felt surreal. Our main financial goal was to pay off our home before we turned 40. Just after my 36th birthday, the balance in our offset account exceeded our mortgage amount. When you log in to your internet banking, most banks give you a 'total' figure under your accounts. For the first time since buying a home, it showed a positive number. We had more cash than debt.

It was on my 30th birthday that we gave ourselves the challenge of paying off our home loan in 10 years or less. First, we reverse engineered our mortgage using an online repayment calculator and figured out how much extra we needed to pay towards our mortgage each month to shave 20 years off the life of our loan. Then, we came up with three actions to achieve our goal:

1. Refinance to minimise our interest rate.

2. Maximise our household income.

3. Make extra payments into our offset account.

It sounds kind of simple. But this plan required a combination of discipline and stamina. It took years of working far beyond full-time hours to make those extra payments and a consistent approach towards reviewing our home loan to find the lowest rate on the market. After you buy a home, your goal should be to pay it off as soon as possible. It's the ultimate peace of mind. You will have somewhere to live, rent-free, for the rest of your life.

Creating a plan to become mortgage free is integral to becoming debt free. If we hadn't created and agreed upon our financial goals as a couple, our drive to increase our household income would have dissipated months into the journey. It's so much easier to hit the bullseye when you can see the target.

## Refinancing your home loan

Banks have one major goal: to maximise their profits. They do this by charging you interest on your home loan. To attract new customers, banks will offer competitively low interest rates. But most banks will not pass this low interest rate on to their existing customers. Even if you contacted your bank to ask for the low rate they have advertised online, you'll be met with a representative from their 'customer options team' who has been trained to retain your business with the highest interest rate possible. There's a simple solution. Become a new customer at a different bank.

Some banks are so desperate for your business that they will offer a 'cashback' of up to $3000 once you've refinanced your home loan. Your existing bank is relying on the fact that it's too much hassle to change banks. Back in the day this was definitely the case, but with easily accessible internet banking options at your fingertips, more and more Australians are opting to spread their loans and accounts across multiple institutions. Your goal should be simple: refinance to the bank that charges you the least in interest and fees.

To find the bank with the lowest comparison rate and best cashback offer, reach out to a mortgage broker. My network of mortgage brokers will support you through the process, completely free of charge. Your existing bank will probably charge you a fee to discharge your mortgage, but in most cases these fees are more than paid for by the cashback received from your new bank. Refinancing to a home loan with a lower interest rate will reduce your minimum monthly repayments. This is great if you're struggling to make the minimum repayments on your current mortgage. But remember, this chapter is about becoming debt-free. Don't let lower minimum monthly repayments seduce you. Minimum repayments are designed to keep you paying for 30 years, maximising the interest charged. Instead, you should keep making the maximum repayments possible. A lower interest rate means you'll pay your mortgage off sooner and be charged less interest over the life of the loan.

Table 9.1 demonstrates the impact refinancing can have on the life of a home loan and the interest charged.

**Table 9.1: interest saved after refinancing a home loan**

| Home loan of $600 000 | Existing rate of 7.2% p.a. | Refinanced rate of 6.6% p.a. | Refinanced rate of 6.2% p.a. |
|---|---|---|---|
| Minimum monthly repayment | $4073 | $3832 | $3675 |
| Time to pay off loan making minimum monthly repayment | 30 years | 30 years | 30 years |

*(continued)*

**Table 9.1: interest saved after refinancing a home loan (*cont'd*)**

| Home loan of $600 000 | Existing rate of 7.2% p.a. | Refinanced rate of 6.6% p.a. | Refinanced rate of 6.2% p.a. |
|---|---|---|---|
| Total interest charged over life of loan | $866 183 | $779 504 | $722 933 |
| Time to pay off loan if paying $4073 per month | 30 years | 25 years and 3 months | 23 years and 3 months |
| Total interest charged if paying $4073 per month | $866 183 | $634 084 | $531 660 |

As you can see, if you're on a higher interest rate, keeping your repayments the same after refinancing to a lower interest rate can shave several years off the life of your loan and save you hundreds of thousands of dollars in interest.

# Accelerated payments

One strategy thousands of Australians use to get ahead on their mortgage is to make accelerated payments. You can do this by dividing your minimum monthly repayment in half and paying it fortnightly instead. At a glance, this strategy seems like you're paying the same amount, just fortnightly instead of monthly. However, it makes a massive difference over the life of your loan. This is because there are more than 4 weeks in a month (well, apart from February!), so by making accelerated payments in this way, you end up making one extra monthly repayment per year without even realising it.

To make accelerated payments, this home owner would need to divide their monthly repayments of $3793 by 2 and pay

$1897 instead (rounded up to the nearest whole number) on a fortnightly basis. Figure 9.1 compares the two repayment options based on a $600 000 home loan with an interest rate of 6.5 per cent per year with monthly repayments over 30 years.

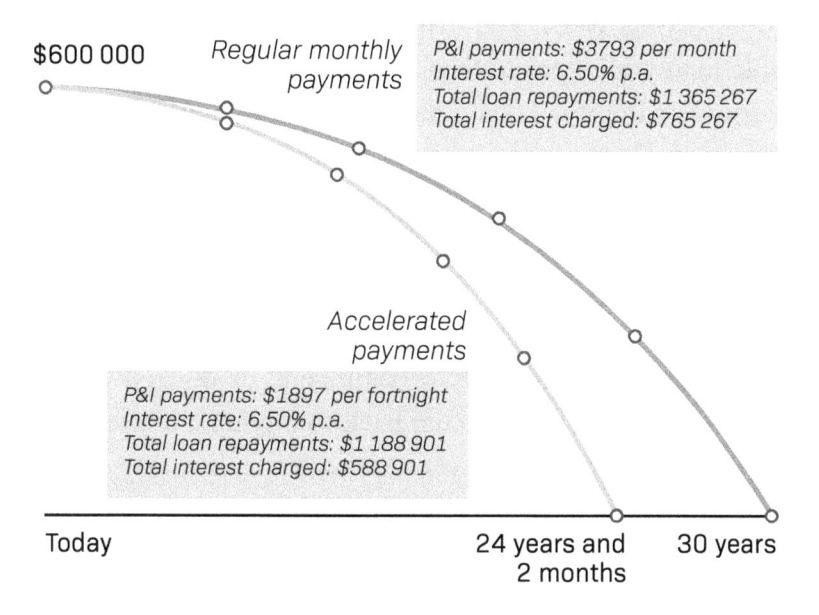

**Figure 9.1: interest charged on a $600 000 home loan making monthly versus fortnightly accelerated payments**

Regular monthly payments
P&I payments: $3793 per month
Interest rate: 6.50% p.a.
Total loan repayments: $1 365 267
Total interest charged: $765 267

Accelerated payments
P&I payments: $1897 per fortnight
Interest rate: 6.50% p.a.
Total loan repayments: $1 188 901
Total interest charged: $588 901

By paying fortnightly, the home owner would pay their home loan off in 24 years and 2 months, shaving 5 years and 10 months off the life of their mortgage. They would also save $176 366 in interest. It's important to note that if you call your bank and ask to pay your mortgage fortnightly, they may recalculate your minimum fortnightly repayments. Making your minimum fortnightly repayments is not an example of the accelerated payment strategy. You must divide your minimum monthly repayment in half and make that payment fortnightly.

# Paying off your mortgage ASAP

You will hear countless finance experts tell you to invest rather than pay off your mortgage because you'll make more money than you'll save in interest. They could be right. They could also be wrong. When you make extra repayments towards your home loan you're guaranteed a return. You're guaranteed to be charged less interest. Likely hundreds of thousands of dollars less in interest. Once you've paid off your home loan and you've secured a place for yourself and your family to live rent-free, then you can start making riskier investments.

But if making extra repayments towards your home loan can literally save you hundreds of thousands of dollars, why isn't everyone doing it? It all comes back to buying a home you can afford. Most first home buyers opt to secure a mortgage based on two full-time incomes, which means they can get caught out if they have kids and one partner stops working. If you want to pay your home loan off in less than 30 years, you need to buy a home at a price point that can facilitate your goal. You might be approved to buy a house in a particular location, but how much sooner could you pay off a townhouse in the same area? If you elect to buy a unit or apartment instead, how will this impact the length of your home loan?

Of course, you want to live in a home where you feel happy. But you also need to consider your age. Remember, the average age of a first home buyer in Australia is 36. A 36-year-old making the minimum repayments on their home loan will still be making those repayments at 60. In fact, they won't be mortgage free until they're 66 years old. Someone making the minimum repayments starting at 45 years of age won't have their house paid off until they're 75. When do you intend to retire? How will you retire while trying to make the repayments on a mortgage? Start considering how your financial decisions today will impact your flexibility in the future.

If a bank has determined that your maximum borrowing power is $800 000 at 6.5 per cent per year, it means you're able to make minimum repayments of $5057 per month. Table 9.2 summarises how much faster you could pay off a range of smaller home loans by making the same repayment of $5057 per month at the same interest rate.

**Table 9.2: impact of making extra repayments across a range of home loans**

|  | Size of home loan | | | |
| --- | --- | --- | --- | --- |
|  | $800 000 | $700 000 | $600 000 | $500 000 |
| Time to pay off loan paying $5057 per month | 30 years | 21 years and 6 months | 15 years and 11 months | 11 years and 11 months |
| Total interest paid over life of loan | $1 020 356 | $597 105 | $363 461 | $217 987 |

If you can afford an $800 000 home, but you buy a $500 000 home instead, you will pay off your mortgage 18 years and 1 month more quickly. If you bought this $500 000 home at the age of 36, you would be completely mortgage free at the age of 47. This is why it's so important to take control of your income before you buy your first home. If you put strategies in place to maximise your income first, then you can choose to buy something below your maximum borrowing power and create a debt-free plan like the one above.

# Keeping up with the Joneses

As you learned in earlier chapters, the difference between your outstanding mortgage and the value of your home is known as your equity. For most home owners, particularly over the past 5 years, home values have increased. So even those who have made the minimum repayments on their home loan have gained substantial equity. A staggering number of home owners choose to increase their outstanding mortgage by refinancing and spend their surplus funds on depreciating assets. A brand new car, camper trailer, boat, caravan, jet ski or motorbike. These are most common purchases I see home owners make after increasing their mortgage by refinancing. They justify their purchases because the interest rate of their mortgage is substantially lower than the interest rate of a personal loan or a credit card would be. But this decision sets them back years. I understand the need to buy a car if your existing one breaks down or becomes unsafe. But you don't need to buy a brand new one. In short: if you need to refinance your mortgage to buy it, you can't afford it.

Let's have a look at an example.

### CASE STUDY

### Xinyu goes on holiday

Xinyu secured a $600 000 home loan back in 2022 at the age of 36 to buy a house for $650 000 in Perth, Western Australia. The house is now worth $875 000. The minimum repayments at 6.5 per cent per annum are $3793 per month. Xinyu has been paying $4425 per month off his mortgage. After 3 years, he has $552 309 outstanding on his home loan. He decides to refinance his home loan up to $700 000, exactly 80 per cent of his home's new value. His bank convinced him to do this so he won't pay LMI. This gives him $147 691, enough to buy a brand new Land Cruiser and go on a trip to Bali. His new minimum monthly repayments on a $700 000 loan are $4425. Let's compare his two home loans.

|  | $600 000 home loan at age 36 | $700 000 home loan at age 39 |
|---|---|---|
| **Amount Xinyu repays each month** | $4425 | $4425 |
| **Time to pay off loan** | 20 years and 6 months | 30 years |
| **Age once loan is paid off** | 56 | 69 |
| **Total interest paid** | $486 334 | $892 812 |

If Xinyu had refrained from using his equity to buy a Land Cruiser and go on a holiday, he would be mortgage free at the age of 56 — well before retirement. Now, he's stuck making his minimum monthly mortgage repayments through his entire 60s. Let's hope he's still able to earn an income that meets his mortgage repayments.

# Exit plan

If you apply for a home loan as a mature-age borrower, you'll need to provide an exit strategy for how you plan to pay off your home loan. The minimum age at which an exit plan is required varies depending on the bank. For example, if you applied for a 30-year home loan at 55, and made the minimum monthly repayments, you wouldn't have it paid off until you are 85 years old. Since this is well into retirement age, the bank needs proof that you will be able to pay off the remaining balance of your home loan at your expected retirement age or continue making your minimum repayments without working. Your exit strategy will depend on your asset position, income and retirement plans. While there isn't a guaranteed strategy accepted by banks, the most commonly accepted exit plans include:

- passive post-retirement income such as rental income, annuities or dividends

- committing to higher repayments to ensure the home loan will be paid off prior to retirement

- committing to downsizing your property after retirement. You will need to outline the suburb, preferred size and price range of the property you plan to purchase during the downsizing process to prove that it's possible based on the expected balance of your home loan

- selling an investment asset such as a property or shares at the time of retirement to pay off your remaining home loan balance

- using the projected balance of your super fund to pay off your home loan in a lump sum once you've hit retirement age.

Strategies that banks don't usually accept are:

- a predicted sale of a business
- future inheritance
- an anticipated workers compensation payout
- predicted employer bonus payments or wage increases
- anticipated family law settlements.

The banks have tight restrictions around exit plans because they want to protect their investment and they know how hard it is to make mortgage repayments once you've retired. You need to treat your retirement the same way. What financial goals are you creating today to safeguard your flexibility and lifestyle throughout retirement?

Let's reflect on how you can plan to be mortgage free.

> **REFLECT**
>
> ## Create your plan for becoming mortgage free
>
> By now, you should know what you can afford. You've learned about the ongoing costs of mortgage repayments as well as the hidden costs of owning a home. You've researched ways to increase your income and forecast what impact this potential income could have on your home loan. Now it's time to create your plan to become mortgage free. How long will it take you to pay off your
>
> *(continued)*

mortgage and how much more will you need to earn to pay it off sooner?

Use an online repayment calculator to answer the questions below based on current home loan interest rates. (I personally think the most user-friendly option is the Commonwealth Bank's. Go to the *commbank* website and search for 'mortgage repayment calculator'.)

- What is the expected size of your home loan?
- What is the expected total monthly cost of owning your home inclusive of mortgage repayments and all hidden costs?
- How much extra per month can you pay towards your home loan?
- How long will it take you to pay off your home loan by making these extra repayments?
- How much interest will you save by making these extra repayments?
- If you can increase your income by $500 after tax per month and pay this towards your home loan, how long will it take you to pay it off?
- If you can increase your income by $1000 after tax per month and pay this towards your home loan, how long will it take you to pay it off?
- If you can increase your income by $2000 after tax per month and pay this towards your home loan, how long will it take you to pay it off?

The last three questions above are the most important. It's this type of thinking that led to me paying off my home loan of over $700 000 in only 6 years. How can I increase my income by $500 per month? What about $2500 per month? What about $5000 per month?

> ### 🏠 EXPLORE YOUR OPTIONS
>
> ## Refinancing
>
> One of the keys to paying off your home loan faster is to secure a mortgage with the lowest possible interest rate. You'll probably need to wait until you have at least 20 per cent equity in your home before you can refinance to avoid being charged LMI. But with house prices continuing to soar across the country, this may be sooner than you think. Make sure you're prepared by completing a table like the one below using a rate comparison website such as *Canstar* (search for 'home loan comparison' and filter by 'refinance').
>
> | Name of bank or lender | Variable comparison rate | Fixed 1-year comparison rate | Fixed 3-year comparison rate | Do they offer cashback? If so, how much? |
> |---|---|---|---|---|
> |  |  |  |  |  |

There is one way to guarantee that it takes you 30 years to pay off your home loan: never refinance your home loan and never increase your income. You'll own your home around the time you retire, but then what? What will your life look like after that? Will you be financially flexible?

I have just transitioned to the next phase of my financially flexible journey. My mortgage is paid off and now I'm focused on building wealth for my family. My goal is to build a sustainable passive income so I can retire whenever I need or want to. Increasing my income was step 1. Buying my first home, step 2. Paying off my mortgage, step 3. Now it's time to set myself up for life. I'll show you how in chapter 10.

## CASE STUDY

## Luke and Zoe's home-buying journey

Luke and Zoe bought their first house in Sydney in 2015 for $750 000 at the ages of 30 and 29 respectively. They were both working fulltime, and their parents helped looked after their two children to reduce the cost of day care. After living in the property for a year, Luke and Zoe, both teachers, decided to relocate to a rural town in New South Wales with their kids. Both secured teaching positions at the local school and they planned to stay there for 2 years.

### *Luke and Zoe's financial snapshot*

| | | | |
|---|---|---|---|
| **Luke's annual before-tax income** | $131 000 | **Parent guarantor** | Yes |
| **Zoe's annual before-tax income** | $78 600 | **Monthly living expenses** | $1000 due to subsidies |
| **Total annual before-tax income** | $209 600 | **Total credit card limits** | $0 |
| **Job title** | Teachers | **Monthly personal loan repayments** | $0 |
| **Total savings** | $67 500 at the time of purchase | **Monthly student debt repayments** | $0: all student loans paid off |
| **Eligible for government support** | Yes | **Residency status** | Australian citizens |

## *Luke and Zoe's outcome*

After making the move, Luke and Zoe decided to rent out their house in Sydney. Their goal was for the rental income to pay a majority of their mortgage while they were away. They both received an increase in salary for working in a rural location as well as housing subsidies, including a 50 per cent discount on rent and utilities. Since they no longer had the support of their parents, Zoe reduced her workload from fulltime down to 0.6 FTE, working 3 days a week.

After adjusting to their new lifestyle, Luke and Zoe realised they could repay an extra $5300 per month on their mortgage. Their rental income, combined with their reduced living expenses and no liabilities, had a massive impact on their cash flow.

After 2 years, Luke, Zoe and their kids loved living rurally so much that they decided to stay. Now, 8 years later, as their kids are becoming teenagers they are planning to move back to Sydney. While living rurally, they consistently paid an extra $5300 per month towards their mortgage. In only 9 years, they have fully paid off their mortgage. Now they are faced with a decision: move back into their family home debt free, sell this home and use the profits to upgrade their home or use the equity to buy an investment property. Regardless of what they decide, their consistent hard work has paid off.

# Key takeaways for your home-buying journey

- The first step to paying off your home loan as soon as possible is to ensure you have the lowest interest rate on the market.

- If your rate increases to more than what other banks offer, refinance your home loan to a new bank and take advantage of any 'new customer' promotions such as cashback offers.

- The accelerated payment strategy could shave around 5 years off the life of your home loan. Simply divide your minimum monthly repayment by 2 and pay this figure fortnightly.

- Making the minimum repayment of an $800 000 mortgage on a $600 000 mortgage will shave over 14 years off the life of your home loan, so think twice before buying a more expensive home.

- Don't refinance your home loan to release equity to buy depreciating assets. This will set you back years and could potentially cost you hundreds of thousands of dollars in interest.

- If you apply for a home loan as a mature-age borrower—meaning your loan term finishes past the age of retirement—you will need to provide an exit plan. If the bank doesn't believe you'll be able to afford a mortgage while retired, neither should you.

- Create your plan to become mortgage free by investigating how much more you need to pay as extra monthly repayments to be mortgage free in your desired time frame.

# 10 | Achieve FINANCIAL FLEXIBILITY

I became a father just before I turned 30. I remember, on my 30th birthday, having a visceral reaction to the realisation that I'm now responsible for a little human being. My actions directly impact his life. At first, the thought was overwhelming. But after a while it became my fuel. I became fixated on creating a financially flexible life for my family, and paying off our mortgage was only the first step.

For my wife and me, a financially flexible life means:

- paying off the mortgage on our family home as soon as possible (tick). We want to ensure that we aren't a financial burden to our children once they become adults. Securing our mortgage-free family home means we will have somewhere to live rent-free for the rest of our lives

- maximising the time we can spend with our kids at all ages of life. To achieve this, we have had to focus on increasing the hourly rate of our household income rather than our income overall. Even now, after our mortgage has been paid off, I'm still brainstorming ways to increase my hourly rate so I can spend even more time with my family

- being prepared to support our children to buy their first homes when they're ready. If the housing market continues to trend in the same way, it will be unfathomably harder to buy your first home in 20 years from now

- investing now to create a passive income in the future that funds our lifestyle throughout retirement. It's important that this future passive income stream is safeguarded against inflation. It's not just about having cash in the bank

- both of us retiring before we turn 50. We want to be young enough to enjoy the fruits of our labour and limber enough to explore the world.

If you're at the very start of your financial journey, on the precipice of buying your first home, don't shy away from this chapter. Understanding the end goal will help you put your priorities into perspective. It's never too early to create your financial flexibility roadmap — it can only be too late.

## Renting in retirement

The Grattan Institute and the Australian National University revealed a disturbing statistic in 2024: half of all people renting in retirement are living in poverty. The last thing I want to be, throughout any phase of my retirement, is a burden. When you get to a certain age, if you can't support yourself financially, your kids will need to make a tough decision: potentially let you suffer in poverty or support you financially themselves. This might be at a time when they are trying to support their own growing family. It is your responsibility to create a financial plan while you're still working that sustains you throughout retirement.

The problem is that the age pension in Australia doesn't cater for the cost of renting. It's designed to cover the cost of living, assuming you already own a home. Currently, there are roughly 7.5 million Australians renting, and the expectation is that the number of retired renters will double over the next 30 years. To cover rent, their largest expense, these retirees need to utilise their superannuation.

The average super balance at retirement stands at roughly $340 000 for men and $260 000 for women. The Grattan Institute explains that research shows these average numbers are grossly inflated by people who have a very large superannuation balance. The problem is, to cover the cheapest rent of between $15 000 and $20 000 a year, you would need a superannuation balance of around $300 000 at retirement. My fear is that it's going to become harder. My fear is that housing affordability will decrease over time and the cost of living will increase.

I don't want these statistics to scare you. I want them to motivate you. You're reading this book because you want to act. Step 1 was to take control of your income. I hope this chapter makes you realise the importance of steps 2 and 3: buying your first home then becoming debt free. Now let's discuss how I plan to retire before I'm 50 and live off my passive income.

# Increasing your hourly rate

In part I of this book, you learned how to increase your income to save a house deposit and borrow enough money to buy your first home. If you have kids, your time will become more precious. I often found myself stuck between a rock and a hard place: feeling guilty that I wasn't with my family when I was working, then feeling like I wasn't doing enough to provide for my family when I wasn't working. I found the perfect solution to this problem: increase my hourly rate.

Let's be clear: this isn't going to happen overnight. I've spent years building a small business, working over 75 hours a week to refine my income streams to a point where I've maximised the hourly rate enough that I can reduce my workload to less than 40 hours a week. I now spend more time with my family than most primary household earners and I believe we can still achieve our goal of financial flexibility.

It's also important to understand that if you don't receive a pay increase by the end of the year, you've technically taken a pay cut. This is because inflation is driving up the cost of goods every month. With annual inflation sitting at around 4 per cent at the time of writing this book, your income would need to increase from $100 000 to $104 000 to simply break even.

Here are five things you should be doing to increase your hourly rate:

- Ask for a pay rise from your current employer. Book a meeting to discuss the steps needed to obtain a pay increase.

- Never stop refining your resume or researching new employment opportunities. Depending on your industry, it might be worth signing up with a recruitment agency to secure a higher paying role.

- You should always be learning something new. Whether that's increasing your skill set within your current space to move up the ladder or learning an entirely new skill set with the hope of transitioning into an entirely different industry. Reverse engineer the process by finding a higher paying job first. Research the required qualifications, then find relevant training opportunities. It's important to know where your extra training can lead you.

- Don't be afraid to start a side hustle in addition to your full-time job. I'm not going to sugar coat it: small-business ownership is challenging, and it will definitely lead to you working more hours per week in the beginning, but your hourly rate has the potential to skyrocket compared to solely working as an employee.

- Consider working non-standard hours in a second job to earn an increased hourly rate while reducing your workload from your full-time job. A friend of mine used to work fulltime earning $35 per hour. He asked to reduce his workload down to 4 days a week, working Monday to Thursday. On Monday, Tuesday and Thursday nights he works a second job for 3 hours a night, earning $70 per hour. This has increased his average hourly rate from $35 to $42.68. He now works 1 extra hour a week than he did previously but has 3 full days off per week!

# Generating a passive income

My goal is to retire at 46. Well, not entirely. I really love what I do for work. So, at this point in time, I can't ever see myself retiring. But, by the time I hit 46, I want the option to retire. I want our entire life to be funded by passive income streams so I can choose to semiretire or fully retire as I see fit. I'm 36 now and this year we paid off our mortgage completely. The most common reaction I received from those closest to me was one of celebration coupled with relief: 'Well done! It must feel great not having to make those mortgage repayments anymore?'

But I have worked hard for the past 10 years, consistently increasing my hourly rate so I could pay off my mortgage more than 20 years early. So now what?

I came home from the office one day recently and presented this plan to my wife: let's use the equity we now have in our home to buy an investment property. In fact, let's buy multiple investment properties. We'll use the rental income to pay a majority of the mortgage and contribute the same amount each month we had been repaying off our own mortgage. From a cash-flow perspective, it means nothing has changed: our out-of-pocket expenses are the same as they were when we were making extra repayments on our family home, but it means that in 10 years from now we will own these investment properties outright. The rental income from these investment properties will fund our life.

These are the steps we took to build our investment portfolio:

1. First, we refinanced our existing home loan by getting our house revalued. We were then able to redraw up to 80 per cent of our home loan without needing to pay for LMI.

2. Next, we needed to find an investment property to purchase. We opted for a newer property—less than 8 years old—on a decent-sized block in a desirable suburb, close to where we currently live. The amount we receive in rent for this property as a percentage of its value is lower than other properties for sale, but it has a higher likelihood of appreciating in value based on its location.

3. To purchase the property, we redrew just over 20 per cent of the investment property's value against our family home. This resulted in two home loans: one of just over 20 per cent of the investment property's value secured against our family home and the other at 80 per cent of the investment property's value secured against the investment property itself. This structure maximises our ability to reduce our taxable income by claiming the interest charged by the bank on both loans. It means we didn't need to contribute any cash to make the purchase and we weren't charged LMI.

4. We chose a riskier option for our second investment property. To maximise our expected rental income and offset the low rental yield on our other investment

property, we bought in a coastal town renowned for its holiday homes. Our goal is to utilise the property as a holiday home for our own family a few weeks of the year, while renting it out on a weekly basis for the remainder of the year. This decision was not made lightly as it does attract higher fees from holiday rental management agencies compared to property rented out on a long-term basis. We also run the risk of it being vacant more often than we'd like.

We repeated the same loan structure for this property as we did for our first investment property. An additional home loan of just over 20 per cent of the investment property's value is secured against our family home and a loan of 80 per cent of the investment property's value is secured against the investment property itself.

This strategy only worked for us because our borrowing power had been drastically increased after paying off the mortgage on our family home. The combined rental income from these properties — after management fees, ongoing costs and taxes — should fully fund our lifestyle in 10 years' time. If you decide to purchase an investment property while paying your existing mortgage, your income will need to be high enough to service both loans. You will also need enough equity in your existing home to use as a deposit for your investment property purchase.

Figure 10.1 outlines our current home-loan structure.

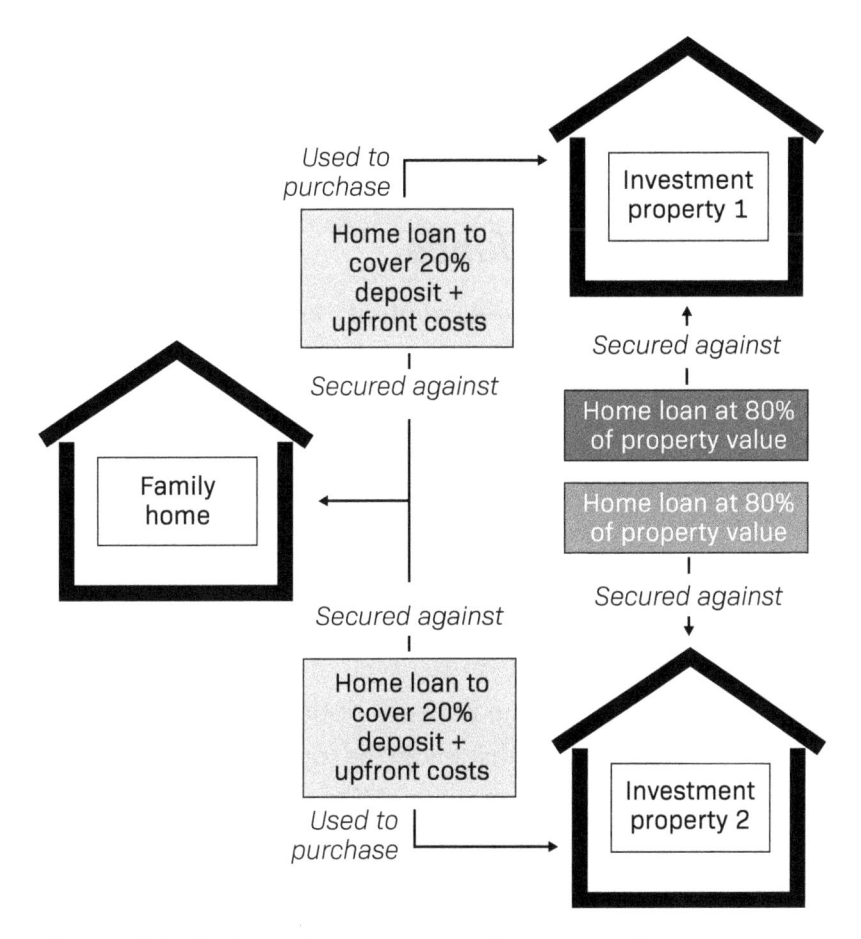

**Figure 10.1: the home loan structure of my properties**

## Investing in the stock market

I've said this several times already in this book, but boy do I wish I had a crystal ball. It would make picking individual companies to invest in so much easier. To be honest, I know very little about selecting the right companies to invest in. This is mainly because I don't have the time to research all the options. I do, however, understand that diversifying where I invest my money

Achieve financial flexibility 219

is important. I don't want all my eggs in the investment property basket. This is why I've taken the simplest approach possible to investing in the stock market.

## Exchange traded funds

An exchange traded fund — commonly known as an ETF — is a pooled collection of assets that tracks a specific index, sector or commodity. I choose to invest most of the money I have allocated to the stock market into a basket of assets rather than investing it in shares in a single company. ETFs can be bought and sold on stock exchanges all over the world, just like regular stocks. So how do I decide which ETFs to buy?

ETFs will vary depending on the type of index they track, the sector they focus on and the level of risk they carry. For example, you could choose an ETF that tracks the top 300 companies listed on the Australian Stock Exchange (ASX). Or you could opt for an ETF that tracks the top 100 companies in the world, excluding Australia. In addition to finding an ETF focused on a particular sector, I like to review its history, analysing its performance and longevity. The last element I consider is the management fee. You'll find that some ETFs have a history of average returns with very high management fees. If you aren't getting the return, what are you paying for? A reasonable management fee sits somewhere between 0.07 per cent and 0.2 per cent per annum.

## Dollar cost averaging

Dollar cost averaging is the practice of investing a fixed dollar amount on a regular basis, regardless of the share price. It was first coined by Benjamin Graham in his book *The Intelligent Investor*. By investing a fixed dollar amount, your money buys fewer shares when prices are higher, and more shares when prices are lower. I use this strategy to reduce market timing risk. Rather than fixating on the market and trying to time it perfectly, I invest the same amount each month, so I don't have to worry about market volatility. My strategy in the stock market is all about keeping it simple and stress free.

You most likely already practise dollar cost averaging via your superannuation. Your employer automatically sends a percentage of your salary to your superannuation account. This money is then invested into ETFs, managed funds and individual companies. Dollar cost averaging ensures you invest consistent, regular amounts regardless of how markets are performing.

## Maximising your super fund

Another way to safeguard your lifestyle in retirement is to maximise your super fund. The first step to making sure you have the most money sitting in this account at the time of retirement is to choose a fund with low fees. Table 10.1 details the difference in retirement balance between 1.00 per cent and 1.5 per cent in management fees.

**Table 10.1: how super fund management fees can affect your bottom line**

|  | Scenario 1 | Scenario 2 |
|---|---|---|
| **Starting age** | 25 | 25 |
| **Retirement age** | 67 | 67 |

*(continued)*

**Table 10.1: how super fund management fees can affect your bottom line (*cont'd*)**

|  | Scenario 1 | Scenario 2 |
|---|---|---|
| **Starting gross annual income** | $77 948 | $77 948 |
| **Starting balance** | $25 096 | $25 096 |
| **Average investment returns** | 6.85% | 6.85% |
| **Fees as a percentage of balance** | 1.00% | 1.50% |
| **Average life insurance premium** | $194 | $194 |
| **Account balance at retirement** | $795 339 | $689 683 |
| **Difference in retirement balance** | – | –$105 656 |

*Source:* Canstar, 2024, 'How to choose a super fund'.

The second step is to maximise your contributions. As of 1 July 2024, your employer is required to pay 11.5 per cent of your ordinary time earnings into your superannuation. This is scheduled to increase to 12 per cent on 1 July 2025. So, for someone earning $100 000 per year, their employer would contribute $11 500 into their superannuation annually. This is financially beneficial as you only have to pay a concessional tax rate of 15 per cent on these contributions if you earn under $250 000 a year. If you earn more than $250 000 a year, these contributions are taxed at 30 per cent.

In addition to your employer contributions, you can also make before-tax personal contributions totalling no more than $30 000 per year. The more you contribute and the earlier you contribute it, the more money you'll probably have in your account at retirement. However, in most cases, this money will only be available to you once you reach your preservation age. This is between the ages of 55 and 60, depending on when you were born, if you're no longer working or once you reach the age of 65, even if you're still working. Table 10.2 details when you can access your super if you're no longer working.

**Table 10.2: age when you can access your super if you aren't working**

| Your date of birth | Age you can access your super (preservation age) |
|---|---|
| Before 1 July 1960 | 55 |
| 1 July 1960 – 30 June 1961 | 56 |
| 1 July 1961 – 30 June 1962 | 57 |
| 1 July 1962 – 30 June 1963 | 58 |
| 1 July 1963 – 30 June 1964 | 59 |
| After 1 July 1964 | 60 |

Source: moneysmart.gov.au, (n.d), 'Getting your super'.

Think of extra contributions into your superannuation as a locked-in savings plan for retirement. It's going to be great when you get to your preservation age. But it's important to also invest in other assets, such as stocks and properties, that you can access prior to your retirement.

## How we distribute our income

My wife and I allocate a set percentage of our net household income to each of our expense categories (see figure 10.2, overleaf).

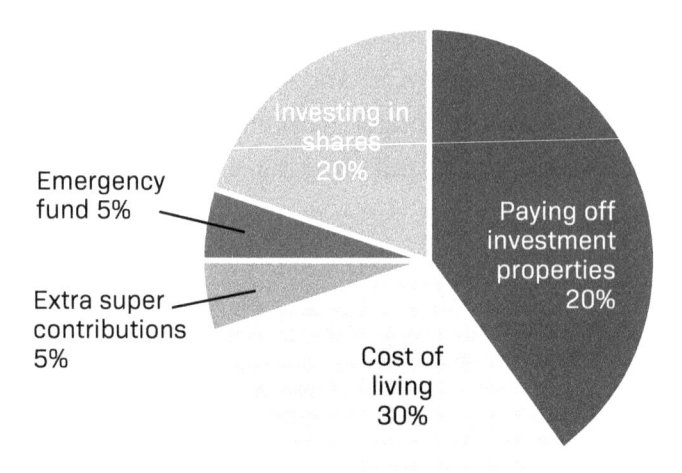

**Figure 10.2: how our income is distributed**

[Pie chart showing: Investing in shares 20%; Emergency fund 5%; Extra super contributions 5%; Cost of living 30%; Paying off investment properties 20%]

Our largest expense, by far, was the monthly repayments made towards our home mortgage (40 per cent of our net household income). Now that our home is paid off, that money is being redirected towards paying off our investment properties.

Since one of our financially flexible goals is to live off the passive income received from our investment properties, we've made it a priority to pay off these mortgages as soon as possible. To make that happen within 10 years, we're contributing 40 per cent of our after-tax income as repayments towards these mortgages.

We pay 30 per cent of our after-tax income towards our living expenses. This pays for all of our essential living expenses, such as utility and grocery bills, as well as our non-essential expenses, such as travel and eating out.

To diversify our investment strategy, we spend 20 per cent of our after-tax income on the stock market. Every month, 20 per cent of our income is used to buy a share of an ETF, regardless of the price. For me, using the dollar cost averaging strategy has nullified any anxiety I have around timing the market.

This leaves us with 10 per cent of our after-tax income. To maximise our super balance at the age of retirement we are contributing 5 per cent of our income, equally distributed, as extra super contributions. We have also recently transitioned to a super fund charging relatively low management fees. The remaining 5 per cent is transferred to our emergency fund. This account gives us access to immediately available cash should an unforeseen event arise.

# Helping your children buy their first home

Gaining financial flexibility is all about having options. You have no idea what the future holds. But you will have an increased ability to navigate this unknown future if you have financial flexibility. Housing affordability in 10, 20 or 30 years from now is one of those unknowns. I hope government intervention makes housing more affordable. But if that doesn't happen—if it goes in the opposite direction—how will your children buy their first home? Paying it forward should be a key element of your financial flexibility plan. There are several ways you could help your children enter the housing market:

- *Let them live with you, rent-free, as long as they need to.* Some people believe that forcing your kids to leave the nest when they turn 18 builds independence. I think this couldn't be further from the truth. Give your kids the opportunity to experiment with different careers, explore the world and, most importantly, save what they would otherwise spend on rent. This might give them enough of a leg up to then enter the housing market without any further support.

- *Build an ancillary dwelling on your property.* With many cities facing a rental crisis, local governments all over Australia have made it easier to build a second dwelling on your property. More commonly known as 'granny flats', this type of accommodation could be used as housing by your children as they enter adulthood. It gives your children, their potential partner and even a growing family a place to live, rent-free, while they save their own house deposit. It also gives you space to enjoy an emptier nest, since you're not all under the same roof.

- *Become their guarantor.* You could help your children buy their first home with absolutely no savings in the bank if you've built up enough equity. This would mean that between 20 and 30 per cent of their property purchase would be secured against the difference between your outstanding mortgage and the value of your home.

- *Allow your children to live in your investment property rent-free or at a reduced price.* This will give them freedom to live on their own in their 20s or 30s while increasing their chances of saving their own house deposit. The outstanding mortgage on this property will dictate the burden it places on you as the home owner. In this scenario, however, you will still have the added benefit of reducing your taxable income by the interest charged on the home loan balance.

- *Gift them the deposit.* Draw cash from one of your investments and transfer it to your child before they get preapproved for a home of their own.

Many of the options above have something in common. How can you reduce your child's biggest expense when they become adults—that is, the amount they spend on rent? Your children are your legacy, and the financial decisions you make today should reflect this ideology. That's why I'm working hard now to give my family financial flexibility in the future.

### EXPLORE YOUR OPTIONS

## Investment property research

If you've already bought your first home, you might be closer to buying an investment property than you think. You could utilise the equity in your existing home to use as a deposit to buy your first investment property, pending your maximum borrowing power. While you could benefit from capital growth using this strategy, it's likely to return negative cash flow—in other words, the rent won't cover the costs. This means you would need to be willing to reduce the amount you could make as extra repayments on your family home to offset the cost of owning an investment property instead. This in turn means a longer road to paying off your family home. Only you can weigh up whether it's worth the risk.

If you do want to research investment properties, use a real estate site such as realestate.com.au to find some properties. Here's a list of questions to answer for each property you research.

- What is the address of the property?

*(continued)*

- What is the asking price?
- How many bedrooms / bathrooms does it have?
- If it's a house, what is the size of the block?
- What are the property's main selling points?
- What size do you expect your home loan to be?
- What will the monthly repayments of your home loan be?
- What are the monthly council rates for a home of this value in this suburb?
- What are the expected monthly water rates for a home of this value in this suburb?
- What is the expected monthly building insurance cost for a home of this value?
- What is the expected monthly maintenance cost for a home of this value?
- Are you planning to buy a townhouse, unit or apartment with body corporate or strata fees attached? If yes, what is the monthly cost of these strata fees?
- What would your total monthly costs to own this home be?
- What is the expected monthly rental income of this property?
- What is the expected monthly profit or loss of owning the property (monthly rent minus monthly cost)?

It's important to note that by answering the questions in 'Explore your options' you are working out what your cash flow would be after buying an investment property. You should contact your accountant to discuss the tax benefits of claiming the costs of owning an investment property. This will likely increase the affordability of owning one.

## Creating your financial flexibility roadmap

By acting on everything I've covered in this chapter, you'll create a financial flexibility roadmap for yourself and your family. The earlier you do this, the more likely you will be to achieve your financial goals before you retire.

> **REFLECT**
>
> **Your financial flexibility roadmap**
>
> Your financial flexibility is directly correlated to the opportunities you can provide for your family. But these opportunities won't just fall into your lap. You need to plan for them and, most importantly, you need to act to achieve them. Reflect on the questions below to determine your priorities and create your financial flexibility roadmap.
>
> - What are, or do you expect to be, your minimum monthly repayments on your family home?
> - How much extra per month can you pay towards your home loan?
> - Based on your total repayments, how old will you be when you own your family home outright?
> - To help fund your retirement, do you plan to rely on your super fund?
>
> *(continued)*

- What will be the expected balance of your super fund at retirement age? (Use *Moneysmart*'s online superannuation calculator.)
- Do you aim to retire earlier than your preservation age?
- If so, how do you plan to pay for your life prior to accessing your super?
- Do you currently have or plan to have children?
- If so, how do you plan to help them enter the housing market?
- All of this hinges on you increasing your hourly rate, at least in line with inflation. How do you plan to do this?

For my wife and me, financial flexibility means we have a greater number of options available to navigate the unknowns of life. Our financial flexibility roadmap includes paying off our family home; increasing our hourly rate to spend more time with our children; building a passive income by investing in property and the stock market to fund an early retirement; safeguarding strategies to help our children buy their first homes; and making extra contributions to our superannuation to harvest after our preservation age.

## CASE STUDY

## Anthony and Maria's home-buying journey

Anthony bought his first property in Brisbane at the age of 25, while still living with his parents in Melbourne. It was located near a popular university, maximising the expected rental income of the property. During the next 3 years, Anthony moved out of home, opted to rent an apartment near his work and decided to buy a second investment property in Hobart.

At the age of 31, Anthony met now wife, Maria. In no time, they moved into a new apartment together, choosing to rent closer to the CBD. They decided to buy their third investment property, this time in Perth. Now Anthony and Maria, at the ages of 37 and 33 respectively, have decided to build a home suited to their family of four.

### Anthony and Maria's financial snapshot

| | | | |
|---|---|---|---|
| Anthony's annual before-tax income | $170 000 | Parent guarantor | No |
| Maria's annual before-tax income | $0 | Monthly living expenses | $3500 |
| Total annual before-tax income | $170 000 | Total credit card limits | $6000 |
| Job titles | Anthony: Real estate agent<br>Maria: Stay-at-home mum | Monthly personal loan repayments | $0 |
| Total savings | $510 000 | Monthly student debt repayments | $0 |
| Eligible for government support | No: not first home buyers | Residency status | Australian citizens |

*(continued)*

## Anthony and Maria's outcome

To maximise their savings, Anthony and Maria decided to sell their Brisbane and Hobart properties. After paying off the respective mortgages, real estate fees and capital gains tax, they had a combined profit of $510 000. They decided to keep their investment property in Perth, with a mortgage of $490 000, as it's producing a strong rental yield and they predict the housing market will continue to increase at a higher rate than other capital cities.

This scenario leaves them with a borrowing power of $367 000. They found a block of land 45 minutes from Melbourne's CBD and have chosen to build a four-bedroom, two-bathroom house on the property, all up for $750 000. Once the home is fully constructed, they will have a home loan of approximately $280 000 with repayments of $409 per week. They plan to make extra repayments on their mortgage of $500 per week, resulting in a paid-off mortgage in 7 years and 6 months.

They want to keep their investment property in Perth, using the rental income to pay the mortgage and ongoing costs until it is also mortgage free. Anthony plans to semiretire in his early 50s and use the passive income from the Perth property to fund a portion of their life.

## Key takeaways for your home-buying journey

- Financial flexibility will give you more options to navigate the unknowns of life.

- A financial flexibility roadmap includes such things as paying off your family home as soon as possible, increasing your hourly rate, investing in property and the stock market to build a passive income, and making extra contributions to your superannuation.

- Half of all retiree renters in Australia are living in poverty. Ensuring you own your home before retiring will reduce the likelihood you become a financial burden on your family.

- With current inflation figures sitting at 4 per cent, it's important to brainstorm ways to increase your income each year — otherwise you're technically taking a pay cut.

- You could secure a future passive income by investing in property, then using the rental income to pay a majority of the mortgage. Once this is paid off, you could use the rental income to fund a portion of your life.

- You could also invest in the stock market to take advantage of compounding capital growth over time. The earlier you start, the greater the likelihood you will make serious gains.

- Maximise your super fund by finding a low-cost provider and making extra contributions. This will drastically increase your balance by the time you hit your preservation age.

- If you are financially flexible, you can help your children buy their first home by letting them live with you rent-free, becoming their guarantor, letting them live in an investment property for reduced rent or gifting them part of the deposit for their own home.

- The earlier you create your financial flexibility roadmap, the more likely you are to achieve your goals before you retire.

# CONCLUSION

## THE SECRET TO SUSTAINING A FINANCIALLY FLEXIBLE LIFE

Even though I'm now in a great position financially, I'd still go back and change everything. For most of my 20s I felt suffocated by debt. Powerless to break free from the uninformed financial decisions I made earlier in my life. My pressure cooker of a situation forced me to take control of my income. It was either that or I lost everything. I want you to learn from my mistakes. I want you to avoid the pain. Take control of your income first, before you commit to one of the biggest purchases of your life.

As it stands, someone earning the median income in Australia cannot borrow enough money from the bank to buy an average house. You need to become above average. Creating a budget in line with increasing your income will help you manage lifestyle creep and save for a house deposit. But, with the cost of living and property prices in Australia continuing to skyrocket, you need to put this budget in place now while the dream of owning a home is still alive.

For most people, earning more money means working more hours. But once you've adjusted to a new level of income, you'll start making financial decisions that lock you into this lifestyle. So, you need to ask yourself, 'Is this sustainable?' Instead, you could focus on increasing your hourly rate by strategically negotiating your salary with your current employer. Reviewing your income and creating shared goals with your employer to achieve a pay rise should become a consistent element of your annual performance review. If you're worth more to another employer, then it's time to jump ship, but before you apply for a new job, optimise your cover letter and resume so they exceed their expectations. Prove to your new employer that you're worth even more than what they're prepared to pay you.

Your maximum borrowing power is the first hurdle to buying a home. How much do you have left over after paying for living expenses and liabilities? Debt stacking is an effective strategy to pay off your existing debts to increase your borrowing power so you can enter the housing market. The earlier you can buy your first home, the younger you'll be when it's completely paid off. You'll need to save enough money to pay for your house deposit plus the upfront costs. But knowledge is power, and in this case, your understanding of the government's first home buyer incentives, help-to-buy schemes, first home owner grants and parent guarantor home loans will save you tens of thousands of dollars.

Right now, across most cities in Australia, it's a seller's market. This means your offer to purchase a home needs to be competitive. To strengthen this offer, you'll need to get a home loan preapproval first. It's important to reach out to a mortgage broker to help you find the home loan best suited to your needs. Don't waste your time on hold to 20 different banks trying to understand their lending guidelines when a mortgage broker will do it for you for free.

Before you take the leap, you need to make sure you can afford the home you want to buy. Budget for the hidden costs and investigate different property types across a range of locations. What type of home can you buy in a regional location? How does this compare to something interstate?

If you manage your mortgage correctly, you'll shave years off the life of your home loan and potentially save hundreds of thousands of dollars in interest. The first step is to ensure you always have the lowest possible interest rate. Most banks only offer their lowest rate to new customers. To solve this problem, refinance your home loan to a new bank to take advantage of this low rate. Making accelerated payments by dividing your minimum monthly repayment by 2, and paying fortnightly, is the simplest way to pay your home loan off sooner. Remember, it's all about making financial decisions you can sustain. This strategy makes it feel like you're repaying the minimum amount when in reality you're making a whole extra monthly repayment each year.

Many investment gurus will pick apart my financial flexibility roadmap, encouraging me to invest earlier, take on even more debt or make riskier investments. I have no doubt that there are ways to make more, but my goal is to make enough. Enough to provide for my family. Enough to live in a desirable location. Enough to help my kids enter the housing market themselves. Enough to self-fund a comfortable, early retirement.

Small-business ownership changed my life. It allowed me to fully take control of my hourly rate. While it's one of the most challenging roads to travel and—at times, it exhausted me mentally—it made me accountable on a level I've never experienced before. I had to sacrifice a lot of time in the beginning, often working 75 hours or more a week. But now, I'm earning what I'm worth and I have the time to give back to my family.

The first step to gaining financial flexibility is to define what 'enough' means to you. No-one knows what's around the corner, but gaining financial flexibility will give you and your family more options to navigate these unknown phases of life.

The secret to creating and sustaining financial flexibility is to create your roadmap, refine your hourly rate and follow through on your commitments. Knowing where the target is makes it so much easier to hit the bullseye. When you work hard for something you don't believe in, you'll become stressed. When you work hard for something you do believe in, you'll become passionate. Passion isn't a starting point, it's a result. Put in the effort and sacrifice now to build the life you and your family deserve.

# Get supported now

There is so much to learn about buying your first home that I've literally written a book about it. Building a team of professionals you can rely on to bring your dreams of home ownership to life is an integral part of the process.

Head to the website below to be connected with one of my mortgage broker, building broker or investment broker referral partners who can support you through your home-buying journey. They can help you create a plan, obtain preapproval from the bank and most importantly answer all your questions.

**www.trustedfinance.loans**

# INDEX

ABS statistics, 3
accelerated payments, 196–197, 237
ACT. *See* Australian Capital Territory (ACT)
ACT Revenue Office website, 135
after-tax income, 76, 224–225
annual income, 3, 5–6, 46
apartments, 178
Australian Bureau of Statistics (ABS), 77
Australian Capital Territory (ACT)
   First Home Owner Grant in, 120
   stamp duty, 134–136
Australian National University, 212
Australian Stock Exchange (ASX), 220
Australian Taxation Office, 135
average house, average income *vs.*, 4–11
average income
—affordable home, 9–11
—*vs.* average house, 4–11
—financial flexibility, 4
—goals, industry that suits, 11–14
—highest paid jobs, 12–13
—home loan borrowing power, 4
—median income, 3
—Situation, Action, Outcome method, 13–14

Basic Budget
—breakdown, 22–24
—household expenditure measure, 24–25
—lifestyles, 25–26
—needs, wants and savings, 22, 24
—percentage targets of, 29
—*vs.* spending habits, 23–24
'best interest duty' policy, 149
body corporate fees, 173–174
borrowing power, for home loan
—debt stacking, 85–87
—income *vs.* expenses and liabilities, 76
—interest rates, 84–85
—investigation, 87–88
—liabilities, 78
   Buy Now Pay Later debts, 82–83
   credit cards, 81–82
   personal loans, 78–81
   student loans, 83–84

borrowing power, for home loan (*continued*)
— living expenses, 77–78
— maximum, 5–6
— overview of, 75
buyer's housing market, 147
Buy Now Pay Later (BNPL) debts, 82–83

case study
— Anthony and Maria's home-buying journey, 231–232
— Bazza's extra tax, 44
— Caitlin's home-buying journey, 165–166
— Chloe's home-buying journey, 15–16
— Daniel and Emma's home-buying journey, 68–70
— guarantors home loan, 122–123
— Jamal's home-buying journey, 48–50
— Josh and Sarah's home-buying journey, 187–188
— Lin's home-buying journey, 89–90
— Luke and Zoe's home-buying journey, 206–207
— Matt and Sahanika's home-buying journey, 33–34
— Victor and Priya's home-buying journey, 141–143
construction loans, 161–162
cost of living, 37

— Basic Budget, 22–26
— classification of, 19–20
— defined, 19
— essential *vs.* non-essential expenses, 20–22
— lifestyle creep, 26–29
— money goal, 29–33
council rates, 171–172
COVID pandemic, 151–152
credit cards, 81–82

debt stacking, 236
— creating, 86
— defined, 85–86
— procedural steps, 86–87
DINKS. *See* double income no kids (DINKS)
dollar cost averaging, 220–221
Doran, George T, 60
double income no kids (DINKS), 169–170
— to parents, 42–43
dwelling purchase
— apartments, 178
— houses, 175–176
— townhouses, 176–177
— units, 177–178

entertainment, lifestyle creep, 29
equity, 200–201
essential expense, 20
— *vs.* non-essential expenses, 21–22
exchange traded fund (ETF), 220, 221, 225

exit plan, to pay off home
    loan, 201–206
expenses
    —essential, 20–22
    —income vs., 76
    —living, 77–78
    —non-essential, 20–22
expensive life. *See* cost of living

Family Home Guarantee (FHG)
    —advantage of, 102
    —description of, 101
    —property price caps, 102–103
Ferriss, Tim, 45
FHBG. *See* First Home
    Guarantee (FHBG)
FHG. *See* Family Home
    Guarantee (FHG)
FHOG. *See* First Home Owner
    Grant (FHOG)
financial flexibility, 4
    —children enters housing
        market, 225–229
    —description of, 211–212
    —hourly rate, 214–315
    —income distribution, 223–225
    —passive income
        generation, 216–219
    —retirement, renting
        in, 212–213
    —roadmap, 229–230, 237
    —stock market, investing
        in, 219–221
    —super fund, maximising,
        221–223

—sustainability, 235–238
—website, 238–239
*finder.com.au*, 20
First Home Guarantee (FHBG),
    97–98, 138–140, 170
    —advantages, 98
    —property price caps, 98–99
    —renewal of, 100
First Home Owner Grant
    (FHOG), 108, 138–139, 170
    —Australian Capital
        Territory, 120
    —New South Wales, 109–111
    —Northern Territory, 120–121
    —Queensland, 113–114
    —South Australia, 117–118
    —Tasmania, 118–119
    —Victoria, 111–112
    —Western Australia, 114–116
fixed interest rates, home
    loan, 153–155
FY23/24 Hayes Salary
    Guide, 61–62

Godin, Seth, 46
Government home-buyer programs
    —Family Home
        Guarantee, 101–103
    —First Home Guarantee,
        97–100
    —First Home Owner
        Grant, 108
        Australian Capital
            Territory, 120
        New South Wales, 109–111

Government home-buyer programs (*continued*)
- Northern Territory, 120–121
- Queensland, 113–114
- South Australia, 117–118
- Tasmania, 118–119
- Victoria, 111–112
- Western Australia, 114–116
— RFHBG, 100–101
— shared equity schemes, 103–108

Government of Western Australia website, 116, 130
Graham, Benjamin, 221
granny flats, 226
Grattan Institute, 212, 213
guarantor home loans, 121–123

HEM. *See* household expenditure measure (HEM)
hidden costs. *See* ongoing costs, of owning home
Higher Education Contribution Scheme (HECS) debt, 83
Higher Education Loan Program (HELP) debt, 83–84
holidays, lifestyle creep, 28
Home Buyer Concession Scheme, 120
home loan
— borrowing power, 4–6
— buyer's market, 147
— construction loans, 161–162
— deposit, 94
— features, 156

offset account, 158–161
redraw facility, 157–158
— interest rates, 150
comparison, 150–153
competitive, 156
split loans, 155
variable/fixed, 153–155
— non-bank lenders, 162–163
— preapproval, 148–150, 236
— refinancing, 194–196
— repayments, 163–164
— seller's market, 147–148
— structure, 218, 219
hourly rate, 214–315
household comforts, lifestyle creep, 28–29
household expenditure measure (HEM), 24–25, 77
houses, 175–176

income
— average (*see* Average income)
— desired, 65–66
— DINKs to parents, 42–43
— distribution, 223–225
— *vs.* expenses and liabilities, 76
— goals, setting, 59–61
— income-tax myth, 43–44
— journey, 37–38
— overtime *vs.* secondary employment, 44–45
— side hustle, 38–41, 45–48
— supplementing, 37, 41, 44, 47–48
— time diary, 41–42

income-tax myth, 43–44
insurance policy, 172–173
*The Intelligent Investor* (Graham), 221
interest only (IO) payments, 161, 162
interest rates, home loan, 84–85, 150
—comparison, 150–153
—competitive, 156
—split loans, 155
—variable/fixed, 153–155
investment
—property research, 227–228
—in stock market, 219–220
dollar cost averaging, 220–221
exchange traded fund, 220

Kelly, Kevin, 45, 46
key performance indicators (KPIs), 62, 63

lenders mortgage insurance (LMI), 94–97, 121
liabilities, 5, 78
—Buy Now Pay Later debts, 82–83
—credit cards, 81–82
—income *vs.*, 76
—personal loans, 78–81
—student loans, 83–84
lifestyle creep, 38
—description of, 27–28
—entertainment, 29
—holidays, 28
—household comforts, 28–29
—shopping habits, 28
—social life, 28
—transport, 28
living expenses, 77–78
LMI. *See* lenders mortgage insurance (LMI)
loan
—construction, 161–162
—home (*See* home loan)
loan to value ratio (LVR), 93–96
location, to buy home, 179
—dwelling types and locations, 181–182
—moving interstate, 180
—regional areas, moving to, 179–180
LVR. *See* loan to value ratio (LVR)

maintenance costs, of property, 173
marginal tax rate system, 44
median dwelling value, 8
median income, 3, 6
money goal
—description of, 29
—spending *vs.* saving, 32–33
—time frame, calculating, 30–32
monthly living expenses, 5–6
mortgage broker, 76, 141
—home loan, 149, 150
mortgage-free plan, 203–204

mortgage management
- accelerated payments, 196–197
- equity, 200–201
- exit plan, 201–206
- overview of, 193–194
- pay off, 198–200
- refinancing home loan, 194–196

mortgage stress, 170

New South Wales
- First Home Owner Grant in, 109–111
- stamp duty, 124–126

non-bank lenders, 162–163

non-essential expenses, 20
- essential *vs.*, 21–22

Northern Territory
- First Home Owner Grant in, 120–121
- stamp duty, 136–138

Northern Territory Government website, 121, 137

offers, to buy home, 184–186
offset account, home loan, 158–161
'1000 true fans', 45
ongoing costs, of owning home, 171, 237
- affordability, 174–175
- body corporate fees, 173–174
- council rates, 171–172
- insurance, 172–173
- maintenance, 173
- water rates, 172

overtime employment, 44–45

passive income generation, 216–219
passive post-retirement income, 202
personal loans, 78–81
PPR. *See* principal place of residence (PPR)
preapproval, home loan, 148–150
principal place of residence (PPR), 106, 110, 116, 117, 120, 137
problem-solving skills, 58

Queensland
- First Home Owner Grant in, 113–114
- stamp duty, 127–129

Queensland Revenue Office website, 114, 128

RBA. *See* Reserve Bank of Australia (RBA)
redraw facility, home loan, 157–158
refinancing, home loan, 205
regional areas, 179–180
Regional First Home Buyer Guarantee (RFHBG), 100–101
rentvesting, 182–184
Reserve Bank of Australia (RBA), 84, 152–154

resume refinement, 66–68
retirement, renting in, 212–213
revenue NSW website, 111, 125
revenue SA website, 118, 132
RFHBG. *See* Regional First Home Buyer Guarantee (RFHBG)

salary negotiation, 61–62
 —benefits, 63–64
 —employer's goals, 62–63
 —expectations and limits, 62
 —new salary benefits, 63
 —preparing to, 64–65
 —time, 64
SAO method. *See* Situation, Action, Outcome (SAO) method
savings
 —Family Home Guarantee, 101–103
 —First Home Guarantee, 97–100
 —First Home Owner Grant, 108
  Australian Capital Territory, 120
  New South Wales, 109–111
  Northern Territory, 120–121
  Queensland, 113–114
  South Australia, 117–118
  Tasmania, 118–119
  Victoria, 111–112
  Western Australia, 114–116
 —guarantor home loans, 121–123
 —home loan deposit, 94

 —lenders mortgage insurance, 94–97
 —loan to value ratio, 93–94
 —mortgage broker, 141
 —RFHBG, 100–101
 —shared equity schemes, 103–108
 —upfront costs (*See* Upfront costs)
 —weekly savings target, 140, 141
secondary employment, 44–45
secured personal loan, 78–80
self-assessment, living expenses, 77
seller's housing market, 147–148, 236
shared equity schemes, 103–104
 —Victorian Homebuyer Fund, 104–108
shopping habits, lifestyle creep, 28
Situation, Action, Outcome (SAO) method, 13–14, 66–68
small-business ownership, 237–238
SMART goals framework, 60–61
social life, lifestyle creep, 28
South Australia
 —First Home Owner Grant in, 117–118
 —stamp duty, 130–132
split home loan, 155
stamp duty, 124
 —Australian Capital Territory, 134–136
 —New South Wales, 124–126
 —Northern Territory, 136–138

stamp duty (*continued*)
— Queensland, 127–129
— South Australia, 130–132
— Tasmania, 132–134
— Victoria, 126–127
— Western Australia, 129–130
State Revenue Office of Tasmania website, 119, 133
stock market, investment in, 219–220
— dollar cost averaging, 220–221
— exchange traded fund, 220
strata fees. *See* Body corporate fees
student loans, 83–84
superannuation, 213, 221–223
super fund, 221–223, 225
surplus funds, 157

Tasmania
— First Home Owner Grant in, 118–119
— stamp duty, 132–134
time diary, income, 41–42
townhouses, 176–177
transport, lifestyle creep, 28
Trusted Finance, 46, 152

units, 177–178
unsecured personal loan, 78–80
upfront costs, 124
— stamp duty, 124
   Australian Capital Territory, 134–136
   New South Wales, 124–126
   Northern Territory, 136–138
   Queensland, 127–129
   South Australia, 130–132
   Tasmania, 132–134
   Victoria, 126–127
   Western Australia, 129–130

variable interest rates, home loan, 153–155
Victoria
— First Home Owner Grant in, 111–112
— stamp duty, 126–127
Victorian Homebuyer Fund, 104
Victorian State Revenue Office website, 112, 127

water rates, 172
weekly savings target, 140, 141
Western Australia
— First Home Owner Grant in, 114–116
— stamp duty, 129–130
worth to buy home, 53
— desired income, 65–66
— income goals, setting, 59–61
— realising moment, 53–59
— resume, refining, 66–68
— salary negotiation, 61–65